THE RETURN OF CHRISTENDOM

BY

A GROUP OF CHURCHMEN

WITH AN INTRODUCTION BY
BISHOP GORE

AND AN EPILOGUE BY
G. K. CHESTERTON

New York
THE MACMILLAN COMPANY
1922

First published in 1922

NOTE

THOUGH the chapters composing this book have been in every case the subject of careful consultation between the writers concerned, and are in a real sense the fruit of their collaboration, the authors do not claim that their outlook is identical in every detail, and responsibility for statements made and views put forward in each chapter rests with the contributor of that chapter alone.

INTRODUCTION TO THE AMERICAN EDITION

AT a moment when everything has been shaken that can be shaken there are those, honest souls they are, who are asking themselves the question, Is it Christianity that is a failure or merely those who are its exponents? Has Christianity been so shaken that it is tottering to the fall? Are the high ideals and glorious visions of twenty centuries a mere Jack O'lantern mocking us as our feet flounder in the morass of today's confusion?

With sufficient justification we might answer that it is Christianity, and therefore Christ, that is at fault, had Christianity been loyal to the spiritual and moral precepts and example of its Founder in the field of the world for a continuous period in the past by the masses of the population with the result as we see it. The truth of the matter is that the great principles of Christ and His Church stand out in bold and sad relief against the lurid history of the last decade, unshaken and unshakable. At the very instant they condemn us for not having made them the active motive of all life, they beg us to learn our lesson and, as never before, take Christ at His word.

> "It fortifies my soul to know
> That though I perish, Truth is so;
> That, howsoe'er I stray and range,
> Whate'er I do, Thou dost not change.
> I steadier step when I recall
> That if I slip, Thou dost not fall."

It would be unfair for me to quarrel with the title of

this volume of essays, each one of which calls for a fearless application of Christian truth to modern conditions, and all together look with courageous hope to the establishment of the Kingdom of God among men— or, if you please, the return of Christendom. But I find myself wondering whether we can have a return of that which has never wholly been. On the other hand the idea of revival or return is sound provided it does not mean a recalling into being of the naked thought or arrangement or scheme of the past. The ideals of the past, yes. Whatever returns must be contingent for its work on motive and direction. Its form must be its own—related to the past but not merely a revivified past.

It is of the very essence of Christianity that its highest reality lies in the future. It delves into the past, it is true, and mines its jewels, resetting them to suit the times. But its eyes are on the unattained. If I have read these essays aright, the writers have been actuated by this distinctively Christian spirit—the forward look. They have studied the past, with special attention to mediæval times, and recovered for us separate jewels from different centuries, relating them to one another in the simple setting of a common motive and a common purpose. It is for us to live not an incomplete but a catholic life, claiming for ourselves and our day all the noble characteristics, the mystic beauty, the irresistible power which have adorned the individual Christian centuries or epochs but which we would gather into one galaxy of glory for all the people and for all the time. Then is real Catholicity. The vicious habit of referring everything to the Reformation of the Sixteenth Century is the antithesis of Catholicity.

Lest I should appear to underestimate the study of the past on which this book is built, I would make my own those famous lines of Seneca[1] upon the joy and power of fellowship with all the world's yesterdays. "Whatever years have gone before us are to be counted our property." The "noble pioneers in high thinking were born for our benefit and fashioned their lives for our sakes. We are brought to consider things of the greatest worth which have been dug up from darkness into daylight by the effort of others; to no period of history are we forbidden access, and we are admitted everywhere. If by greatness of soul we may pass beyond the narrow confines of human frailty, we have unlimited time through which we may course. We may share in the thoughts of all philosophers. And since the universe allows us to go into partnership with all the ages, why, in this tiny and fleeting state of transition should we not give ourselves whole heartedly to the things which are unbounded, eternal, and to be shared with our betters? . . . Shall we not say that men are engaged upon real duties who wish to be on the most intimate terms with the thinkers of past ages? Every one of these will give you his attention; every one of these will send you away happier and more devoted; no one of them will allow you to depart empty-handed from his presence. They can be found by night or by day, and by any one who wishes. . . . These souls will show you the path to immortality and will raise you to heights from which no one is cast down. . . . Anything will be destroyed by the flight of time; but harm can never come to that which wisdom has hallowed."

All that is true of making friends with the individuals of the past is true of making friends with the Christendom of the past. Each of our writers has done this, some

[1] Ad. Paul. de Brev. Vit. 14f. quoted by R. M. Gummere in his *Seneca The Philosopher and His Modern Message.*

THE RETURN OF
CHRISTENDOM

CONTENTS

INTRODUCTION

THIS volume consists of essays written by a group of men who hold certain principles in common, and who have collaborated[1] so as to give their essays a certain manifest continuity and unity of idea and aim. I shall perhaps best serve the purpose of this introduction if I endeavour to enumerate and describe these principles, which they hold in common, and some consequent conclusions.

1. They are all Socialists[2] in a general sense, that is to say, they are all at one in believing that no stable or healthy industrial or social fabric can be built upon the principle of Individualism, or is consistent with the assertion of an almost unrestricted Right of Private Property. Accordingly, they hold that our present industrial society rests upon a rotten foundation; and that what is needed to remedy the manifest "sickness" of our "Aquisitive Society," is something much more than particular social reforms. There is needed the substitution of a true idea or principle of Society—that is of Socialism in some sense—for the false. What they ask for is such a peaceful and gradual revolution as can only come about if men's minds come to be so fully possessed with a certain

[1] Perhaps I ought to say that the Fifth Essay (Dr. Carlyle's) has been contributed, so to speak, from outside, and that he should not be reckoned as belonging to the group.

[2] Dr. Carpenter prefers to be called a "Co-operationist," while some of the other contributors might choose to describe themselves as "Distributionists." None would accept the description "Socialist" save in its most general sense.

set of ideas, which are now in the air, as that they shall gain compelling or driving power in practical affairs.

2. But as a basis for social reconstruction they entirely repudiate the Marxian materialism, or the doctrine of the inevitable Class War and victory of the proletariat. Human affairs are not governed by mechanical laws and do not move towards necessarily determined conclusions. These writers would appeal to the freedom of the human spirit. If there is no change of spirit among men, the class war might proceed to revolution and to the victory of the proletariat, but it would not really ameliorate the lot of men or give them liberty. It would only substitute a bureaucratic tyranny for a plutocratic: and a revolution leading to disillusionments would bring reaction. Moreover, these writers would repudiate the ideal of Communism and the older ideal of State Socialism, as both of them tending to bureaucracy and tyranny. They demand a form and ideal of society which shall secure for the individual his spiritual liberty, and such rights of "property for use" as this liberty and the maintenance of the family require.

3. They feel the weakness of the Labour Movement in general, and in particular in Great Britain, owing to its lack of dominant and guiding principles, and its consequent incoherence and endless tendency to internal faction and division.

4. They see the root and ground of the ideas of justice and brotherhood and the universal duty and joy of social service only in the Christian doctrine of God, as it was proclaimed by the prophets of Israel and given its completion and universality in Jesus Christ; and as it was entrusted to the Church to constitute the basis of its mission. In every element of this fundamental doctrine —of God, of the Incarnation, of the Holy Spirit, of the

ultimate victory of Christ, of the life eternal—they see some strong guarantee, which exists nowhere else, for the ideas and principles which real social recovery constantly postulates. Nor would they be content with any presentation of religion as a mere system of doctrine. They see the visibly organized Church with its sacramental fellowship as belonging to the essence of the religion of the Incarnation. This organized Church is the Body of Christ. It is His organ and instrument for action in the world. It is commissioned not only to proclaim a truth but to live a social life. It exists not only to teach men the way, but to show it embodied before their eyes. In a word, these writers are both Christians and Catholics.

Thus (5) they do not share the current fear of dogma in religion. I suppose they would admit that the dogmatic spirit may become excessive and tyrannical, and that the dogmatic authority needs the constant challenge of reason. But they perceive both that Christianity is nothing if not dogmatic—that is, that it rests essentially upon a message proclaimed to be divine—and that every continuous human society, if it is to maintain any moral ideal, must rest upon a dogmatic basis, that is to say, it must be able to appeal to a certain groundwork of principles which are taken for granted.

But (6), they do not disguise from themselves the deplorable failure of the Church to exhibit the reality of brotherhood and to stand for its principles of justice and love. If one looks back to the early centuries one sees, indeed, brotherhood really taught and really lived. It was this exhibition of brotherhood that won the reverence of the world in spite of its prejudice against the Christians. And through all the period of the Middle Ages, though it is in vain to attempt to conceal from ourselves the very dark aspects of mediæval practice, yet the Church held Europe in some real recognition of a fellowship, at once supernatural and super-national, to which all men and nations belonged or should belong, and in which all men were bound to justice and to the recognition of their spiritual equality before God. But since the Reformation broke up the visible unity of the Church, and the spirit of individualism both in the churches of the Reformation and in the Catholic church obscured the doctrine of the Kingdom of God on earth, and made the Church appear as little else than a piece of spiritual machinery for saving the individual soul for another world, its social function throughout Europe has been almost forgotten. The fabric of Industrialism was built up in almost all European countries on a basis manifestly anti-Christian, almost without remonstrance from the Church. Now the fabric of Industrialism seeems to be crumbling by its own inherent rottenness, and the cry for reconstruction is heard in all directions, but the principles on which alone reconstruction can be based and the spiritual force of which alone it can be accomplished seem to be lacking. So it is that men of all kinds, however much alienated from "institutional religion" are looking, pathetically enough, towards the Church of Jesus Christ, and asking, in very varied tones of voice, what it can do for them in the Name of its Master; and meanwhile there are signs that the Church is waking from a long sleep and beginning to understand again what it means to pray constantly "Thy Kingdom come on earth."

I detect differences amongst these writers, but if I have read the essays aright, I seem to see this body of common principles and conclusions animating them all, and leading them to make a double appeal, first to the Church to take its principles seriously and to "discern the signs of

the times," and secondly, to the democracy to consider
whether it be not true that there is no security for the
principles to which it is blindly appealing, and no real
hope of social salvation, save in the name of Jesus Christ
of Nazareth, the Son of God.

It is because the point of view of these writers, and the
principles on which their point of view is based, so ur-
gently need presentation to the bewildered world of to-
day, and are in themselves so profoundly worthy of consideration, that I have accepted the undeserved honour
which they have offered me of introducing these essays
to the public.

They seem to me to make an arresting appeal.   Obviously they intend to be provocative and challenging, and
make no claim to completeness of treatment.   They
would wish me, I think, to call attention to this : and I will
give some instances of omission.

There is almost nothing about the international problem.   Yet obviously it is impossible to deal effectively
with social reconstruction or with industrial problems
except on an international basis : and obviously we cannot
even begin to think about the Church without recognizing that it is essentially an international or supernational
society.   These writers assure me that they are not blind
to such considerations or lacking in zeal to emphasize
them.   Only it did not seem to be practicable to deal
with them in these essays.   Again, it is obvious that
essays might have been written on the realization of the
idea of brotherhood in the early Church, and on the system and character of the mediæval Church, and on the
connection between the diffusion of the Reformation doctrines and the rise of Modern Industrialism.   But these
topics have been thoroughly treated or are being treated
elsewhere.

Once more the question may be asked these writers, What in fact is the system and kind of industrial and economic reconstruction which you adumbrate? You reject, it appears, Marxism, Communism, and the older form of State Socialism. What is it then that you contemplate? There are hints given by several of the writers pointing towards Guild Socialism as the goal of their efforts. If I may speak on such a subject, though I am least of all an authority on economics, the advocates of Guild Socialism seem to me to have yet a great deal of thinking to do before they can claim that Guild Socialism is a working proposal. And plainly in the book it is barely hinted at and not definitely proposed. That again is an omission. But books are of different kinds. There are book claiming to be comprehensive, systematic and complete. There are others which set out to be stimulating and suggestive. And the latter have as real a value as the former. And it is because, in the latter category, these essays seem to me to be forcible and appealing, that I commend them to the public.

CHARLES GORE.

THE IDEA OF CHRISTENDOM
IN RELATION TO MODERN SOCIETY

BY

MAURICE B. RECKITT, M.A.

Sometime Editor of *The Church Socialist*

SYNOPSIS

I. In the world of to-day the idea of Christendom is obliterated: it is even absent from the teaching of the Church.

It has been rendered incomprehensible by

1. the subjection of the community to capitalist Industrialism,
2. the distortion of property by plutocracy.

These processes are not fortuitous in their origin; they arose because the mediæval standards of Vocation and Fraternity had been destroyed.

Processes of their decay indicated.

Industrialism testifies "sacramentally" to the moral hideousness of capitalism.

Plutocracy degrades property from a means of livelihood and service into an instrument of avarice.

The worship of gain becomes a religion; its denial and frustration of Christian ideals and claims.

II. The Church, however, has not yet revealed herself as the enemy of plutocracy.

But the opportunity to do so may not much longer remain open to her; for the capitalist system is threatening to collapse from its inherent rottenness.

The War—and the seeming inevitability of further world-wars— has shattered the myth of a beneficient Progress; shattered the stability of international capitalism; shattered the belief in the purely political and disinterested character of the State by disclosing the interdependence of plutocracy and State-power.

All these effects of the War have been confirmed by the nature of the "Peace."

Finally, the result has been shattering to the complacency of thousands: this is not necessarily a bad thing, and may even prove a unique opportunity. Since if plutocracy's dominion holds so little promise, an alternative to it must be sought out and pursued.

Hence men will turn naturally to those who already challenge capitalism—the forces of "Labour."

III. The stability of capitalism is not only impaired by its inherent rottenness and its loss of prestige, but for the further reason that the workers are increasingly organizing to transcend the status to which it condemns them.

In view of Labour's resistance to it, capitalism has no future. Yet Labour, while strengthening its resistance, is bewildered and confused by the possibilities to which its successful opposition points.

It is so because it lacks any constructive Idea adequate to embody and achieve its aspirations, hence it fears to find itself baffled by the very completeness of its opportunity.

Its categories of thought and its spiritual values are fatally entangled with the ideology of capitalist society: this is true of both its reformist and revolutionary sections. Its intellectual subservience to the assumptions of a profiteering "economic science" render it incapable of developing a constructive programme.

Yet the Labour movement is something we cannot disregard and of which we must never despair. For with all its limitations it is

1. A reply to the pretensions of plutocracy;
2. A real democracy;
3. Potentially, an engine of emancipation.

IV. The Labour Movement is not, however, a co-ordinated whole. And the emergence of Bolshevism has accentuated and defined a sharp cleavage between "Labourism" and Communism.

Though it may be at present inevitable that the workers should choose between these two sections, the choice is really one between two evils, for neither possess a true unifying principle. The official Labour formula of "workers by hand and brain," though useful for some immediate purposes, is inadequate.

1. Its classification is quite unreal.
2. It suggests dangers of perpetuating social caste.
3. It implies the acceptance of capitalist criteria as to what constitutes socially valuable work.

Fatal consequence of this. The alliance projected by official Labour is a political unification based on a common antagonism.

It does not promise any secure basis for economic achievement or moral unity.

The Labour programme is still quite inadequate, and its task wrongly envisaged. "Nationalization," "Politicalism," the "Leisure State," enclose its horizon; and its activities are dissipated in industrial agitations within the "vicious circle" of capitalism.

V. Bolshevism attempts to beat capitalism at its own game by mastering and improving upon capitalist methods.

Its unifying principle is the "proletariat"; and the basis of its social policy proletarian dictatorship.

The conception of "proletarianism": its false application of Equality; its subjection of Liberty and Fraternity.

"The circumference of capitalist organization becomes the centre of the new society."

A free social order cannot be evolved from this inhuman distortion.

But the vital objections to Bolshevism do not depend upon political considerations; rather do they arise from its exclusively materialistic interpretation of the governing factors in society past and present.

Illustrations of this in—

1. The Marxian view of History.
2. The idea of "proletarian culture" with its glorification of the machine. "Cultural dictatorship."
3. The attempt to find in psychology a basis for the dictatorship of "efficiency," and a justification for the "sweeping away of democratic lumber" in the name of a "sociological Calvinism."

The "new world" of Communism would be founded on the *old values* of plutocracy.

VI. The limitations of the Socialist idea.

Dangers of its inelasticity illustrated by the failure to draw practical consequences from the moral distinction between "interest" and "profits."

Yet the primary need of the workers' crusade is not any practical programme but the inspiration of an all-sufficing Idea. Only the conception of Christendom can supply this: in it men would find not only an ideal for the whole social order, but one which would restore to the individual the conviction of Vocation and a personal activity that could be offered to the glory of God. This ecclesiasticism can never supply within an antagonistic world order.

It is in this sense that society must "go forward from the Middle Ages," before men had proved unworthy of the ideal of Christendom.

This ideal cannot be immediately recovered; nor after centuries of social apostasy can the full implications of the Faith be made visible to the many while it is preached to them in theological forms.

But by the construction of a new social order, built as a clear challenge to plutocracy, an arena would be gradually created in which all men could come to the realization of the Kingdom of God, to which their efforts were making an infinitesimal, but vital, contribution.

CHAPTER I

THE IDEA OF CHRISTENDOM IN RELATION TO MODERN SOCIETY

I

IF we were to ask what form of words came nearest to uniting those scattered and sundered bodies of men and women, who found in the life and death of Jesus Christ a revelation of the Divine purpose for the world, we should discover them in phrases which composed something that was neither a creed nor a prayer only, but essentially both. The Lord's Prayer is robbed of its great intention if it is used only as a string of individual petitions for the devout: it is the cry—and best of all the common cry—of souls who are citizens of the Lord's Kingdom. Yet a million times a day its clauses are framed by Christian men and women for whom some at least of them can have no immediate practical significance whatever. That God's Kingdom should come in order that His Will might be done in earth thereby, so that even here men might breathe in human society the breath of heaven—for this is the Christian bidden to pray, even before he speaks of his daily bread. What can those words mean to those whose lives show them nothing but a morass of "business" or a wilderness of industrialism, equally surrendered to the dominion of plutocracy? In the world of to-day the idea of Christendom is not even repudiated—

it is obliterated. It is not proclaimed in the market-place to inspire the faint or to confound the proud; it is still more fatally and strangely absent from our Churches, so that the Christian Faith, while it may remain a solace to the weak, seldom reveals itself as a challenge to the strong.

The subjection of the community to capitalist indus-trialism and the distortion of property by plutocracy have made the very conception of Christendom not only un-realizable, but for the majority of men to-day even incom-prehensible. They are not, as many seem to imagine, processes which have come about fortuitously, or for rea-sons which were beyond the power of society to control. They arose because, with the decay of the great mediæval standards of vocation and fraternity, and the consequent corruption of the social institutions founded upon them, nothing remained to preserve the purpose of society as the glorification of God. Society—a harmony of interwoven purposes, communally organized—gave place to the State, with its monopoly of power for the glorification of its rulers, till the heresies of individualism came to take their intellectual vengeance for the suppressed truth of the claims of human personality. The cry went forth for freedom, economic no less than political; but it was a free-dom conceived not as a social means, but as a personal end, an "absolute value," an opportunity for the glorifica-tion of man—or, to be more precise, for the glorification of a certain kind of man. For it was freedom to excel each other without restraint that men were in fact claim-ing, not a freedom to contribute to any common purpose; and this precisely at a time when the opportunity of the energetic and the avaricious was being almost miracu-lously enlarged by discoveries which offered to such men, not only new powers over natural resources, but new and terrible tyrannies over their fellows.   The Industrial Revolution—the most ruthless of all revolutions—carried its devastations across a society that had lost all traces of the old defences of Vocation and Fraternity, which it is only now attempting painfully to restore in their secular forms of Function and Solidarity.

Industrialism could never have taken the hideous forms it has done if mechanical discovery had developed in a society founded on free associations and corporate ideals. As one travels through some "black country," or slum-begirt factoryland, wherein what we count as wealth is distilled (though scarcely shared), the very surroundings seem to testify, as it were sacramentally, to the moral impossibility of plutocracy; we look upon the outward and visible signs of an inward and spiritual disgrace.   Nor is it only the processes of industry, or the status of its poor prisoners, that the triumph of plutocracy has distorted; it has turned property from an institution contributing to social health into a dangerous disease, by transforming the deadly sin of avarice into the haughty virtue of "enterprise." For property has sunk from being a means whereby a livelihood was made in the service of society, into an instrument whereby money and power are amassed by the exploitation of society and the bulk of those who work. Hence "the degradation of the worker follows inevitably from the refusal of men to give the purpose of industry the first place in their thought of it."[1]

Into a social order so compounded how can God's Kingdom come? By what means even can the very idea of Christendom return? Plutocracy (and the capitalist fabric through which it operates) does not merely constitute a force hostile to religion: it *is* a religion.[2] When we

[1] *The Sickness of an Acquisitive Society,* by R. H. Tawney, p. 20.
[2] Our holidays are not fixed by Saints' days or to commemorate

ask at the death of its great devotees how much they died worth, we are inquiring (and often appropriately enough) of nothing else about them than the amount of financial power they had contrived to obtain. Nor is it at death only that this religion enforces its claims, nor by its elect exclusively that it demands to be acknowledged. It disputes with the Church of Christ for the destiny of its children. At the moment when the boy (or girl) in a working-class parish is being urged to make recognition of the tremendous claims made for him at his baptism, he is going forth into a world which by every manifestation of its public life promptly denies and frustrates every one of them, and makes plain his fate as a member of the proletariat, the child of Mammon and the inheritor (if he lives long enough) of nothing but the servile dole of an old-age pension. How can the priest bid the wage-slave commend his vocation to God, or serve faithfully a Fraternity in which he has neither status nor honour? He cannot find these things in his work: but till he can do so, the Church which sends him forth can never rightly be other than a foe to the social order which so tragically engulfs him.

II

The Church, however, has still to reveal herself as the enemy of plutocracy, and it is only with the recovery of the ideal of Christendom that she will be able to stand forth with an ideal worthy of her mission to the world she is called to redeem. But the opportunity is one that may not remain open much longer. The capitalist system, in which plutocracy's dominion is embodied, has for

events from the (truly) rich part of our history, but they are *bank* holidays. The closing of our banks is the one signal that for twenty-four hours we are free." *The Camel and the Needle's Eye*, by A. Ponsonby, p. 30.

long been challenged, more or less ineffectively, by those whom it exploits; but it is not only, nor even mainly, for this reason that its control over society is breaking down. It is threatening to crumble because of its own essential instability, and because—to use the old political phrase in a far more crucial connection—it is "losing the confidence of the country." These tendencies, discernible a dozen years ago, have been enormously accelerated by the War, the more vital effects of which are only gradually becoming obvious. And the more obvious they become, the more shattering we perceive them to be. In the first place the War has shattered the myth of a beneficent and almost inevitable Progress, on which the reformers of nearly every school had previously founded their faith. To those who look deep enough—and there are many already who have done so—it has become clear that the whole of our interdependent civilization is exposed to the liability of war by the very nature of the economic system which so precariously binds it together. Some even are found to declare that the clash of expanding and competing plutocracies, in desperate quest of that "effective demand" which their financial operations result only in extinguishing in their home markets, will be hurled forward into further conflagrations, for which their scientific and mechanical "progress" equips them each year more hideously. It is no "far-off divine event," as the Victorians believed, but rather the imminent and hellish menace of successive world-wars to which the whole capitalist creation moves.

Progress, even in the servile forms in which the Liberal optimists of yesterday conceived it, demands international peace, and not peace only, but international stability. That stability which—so far as it then existed—the War shattered, the formal and nominal peace

succeeding it has not restored. Capitalist industrialism
has lost every veneer of stability; its cosmopolitan fabric is everywhere cracking, and has at many points altogether collapsed. The foreign exchanges and world
markets appear irremediably dislocated: their recovery
seems impossible, since what the recklessness of Pots-
dam began, the recklessness of Versailles would appear
to have confirmed. The Europe of 1914 may have been
a vulgar mansion, none too securely founded, and in a
style little to our taste, but its owners at least succeeded
in keeping the wolf from the door. To-day the ravenous
animal is invited to ransack its dilapidated basements,
while what is left of the family seeks desperately to
imitate its old prosperity in a few rooms on the upper
floor.

When the hope of Progress and the assurance of stability are shattered, what remains of the beliefs by which
men were sustained amid the doubts and difficulties of
pre-war days? Little enough perhaps; but while men
believed in the purely political and essentially disinterested character of the State, and of the Government
through which its powers were administered in the common interest, they felt their feet on solid ground. The
State, at any rate, men felt, did stand for the common
good. State officers could be trusted to act impartially;
by State action social change could be achieved; and the
influence of wealth or commercialism would be power-
less to frustrate or distort any political decision. It
would be too much to say that this creed has been shattered, but it has certainly been undermined by the political tendencies of the last few years, which have revealed
to many, who never before perceived it, the interdependence of plutocracy and State power. It is more than
seventy years ago that the *Communist Manifesto* de-

clared the State to be essentially "but an executive committee for the administering the affairs of the whole bourgeoisie." The description is—at the least—a misleading one, and however true, it was at no time the whole truth; but it has never come to being so near the whole truth in England as is the case to-day.[1] The suspicion of this is steadily gaining ground, and under its shadow many for whom the State and its governors represented an authority which they felt they could safely revere without danger of superstition, find themselves dismayed and at a loss whither to turn for the recovery of that sense of security without which men fall victims to social panic or the apathy of despair.

These effects of the War—and of the Peace—have been shattering indeed; shattering to the complacency of thousands who face "the new world after the War" with disillusion and apprehension, feeling it to be set upon shifting sands. That the complacency of our people should be shattered is by no means in itself a bad thing; indeed it may prove itself the very thing for which the situation is calling—the conviction of social sin, or at least of social failure, which may lead on to new social values.[2] People are feeling, as they have never felt for many centuries, that nothing is too bad to happen: it is the urgent and vital task of those who lift their voice to-day to make people feel that if they do but will it and

[1] Any reader who may be interested to discover what is the view of the present writer as to the true rôle of the State, will find that view set out in *The Meaning of National Guilds* (1920 edition), chapter vii.

[2] At the same time, the writer has no wish to minimize the reality of the danger, which such disillusion as men have experienced certainly creates, in spreading so great a degree of apathy, and even despair, as to make it impossible to mobilize their enthusiasm and activity for any effort towards social change.

work for it, nothing is too *good* to happen. There was
never a crisis that was not also an opportunity. The very
fact that men no longer accept—as till lately they did
almost unanimously accept—the belief that plutocracy
is in the nature of things, in itself offers a great opportunity; for it leads them to reflect that if its further
development is not inevitable, an alternative can be found
and pursued—and, what is more, to suspect that it must
be if society is not to fall into dissolution. Where can
they turn but to those whose challenge to plutocracy has
been already uttered; to the forces of "Labour," who
speak already of a "new social order," though tangled so
closely in the meshes of the old one? On those forces,
then, will fall first the weight of this great opportunity:
and all who have the courage to prepare for change must
ask whether Labour has the true values and unifying
principles which alone can make it great enough for its
task.

III

We have already seen the crisis to which capitalist
industry has come as a result of that inherent instability
which the War has so fatally accentuated, and from the
loss of prestige which it has clearly sustained in the
public estimation. But even if these causes were absent,
its efficiency and even its continued existence would be
threatened for the further one that the workers, on whom
it depends, are increasingly organized not merely to
maintain their status and condition of life, but to transcend that status altogether. The assumption that
"Labour" should be, and can be, expected to remain a
passive instrument for the purposes of wealth exploitation, involves an utter denial of the workers' personality

and initiative, not only individually, but as expressed corporately through their industrial associations, which are condemned to remain irresponsible and divorced from all control (save in certain negative aspects) over the industries they cover. This assumption, however, is one that plutocracy is no longer safe in making; and in view of Labour's resistance to it, the capitalist organization of industry has no future; the theory of the "class-struggle" stiffens into a fact; and the community is in danger of a hopeless dislocation in supply. Yet Labour, confronted by the crisis its resistance has thus contributed to provoke, is bewildered and confused. Condemned as it has been for a century and a half subjection to industrialism, and accustomed only to the rôle of opposition, the workers, called by the urgency of the moment to take the leap from a rebellious passivity to responsible leadership, find themselves almost helpless, and even apprehensive of the very catastrophe which they have so long professed to desire. And they are so because they perceive that without the rapid development of a great alternative, the "destruction of capitalism" will mean the destruction of society.

It is the lack, not of "ideas"—for with these Labour is plentifully spoonfed by its "intelligentsia"—but of an Idea adequate to embody and achieve its aspirations that gives to the less irresponsible sections of that movement the lurking doubt that it may be baffled by the very completeness of its opportunity to triumph. True, its leaders whistle shrilly enough in their political manifestos and industrial orations to keep up the courage of their followers—and their own. But such "public opinion" as tends to sympathize with them is not greatly impressed, and a just suspicion is abroad that while Labour repudiates the moral claims of capitalism, it does not repudiate (and, indeed, has largely failed to appreciate) the mater-

ialist basis on which they are founded. Many of the
spiritual values, and whole categories of thought—
whether reformist or "Bolshevist"—now prevailing in
the Labour Movement are fundamentally similar to those
of capitalism. Labour's projected alternatives to capitalism are not in many vital respects contradictions of its
basis and principles, but either modifications or inversions
of them. Their application would change the architec-
tural plan of society by the introduction of new features
which could not, in fact, be grafted successfully on to the
original structure; or they would destroy the whole and
make what might appear a fresh start. At best, however,
it would be but a fresh start on the same old foundations,
and attempted with the same bricks.

This failure of Labour sufficiently to disentangle itself
from the ideas and assumptions on which plutocracy has
raised its wretched social structure is partly moral (as
will be further made clear in later section), and partly—
and consequently—intellectual. The political philosophy
of Labour (so far as it has one), for all its Socialist
tendencies, rests very largely on the individualist fallacies which gave to the pioneers of capitalism their sanction and their opportunity. The affirmation of rights,
rather than the acceptance of functions, is still too often
made the precarious basis of Labour's claims; and "freedom"—eternally elusive if sought for its own sake—is
imagined as the goal of a new and delicately-elaborated
social order, instead of being understood as the inevitable
by-product of a just one. In more practical respects, too,
Labour is still intellectually the slave of its social governors. The hypotheses on which plutocratic society
founds its operations—many of them illusions, and some
of them monstrous fallacies—still masquerade successfully before the workers in the guise of economic science.

That credit must necessarily be based on securities which only capitalists can offer; that "increased production" must in itself and regardless of its nature inevitably be of economic benefit to the whole community; that purchasing-power should only be distributed in return for work; that the multiplication of machinery is a sign, and even a condition, of economic progress; that prices must for ever serve as the "automatic register of the relation between the supply of goods and the supply of money"; that the worker must continue to receive his remuneration in the form of a wage; all these fatal assumptions, and many others, are accepted almost unquestionably in the Labour movement without a glimpse of the truth that while they remain unchallenged, and even unexamined, no constructive economic policy can possibly be developed capable of countering the dominion which plutocracy, by maintaining such superstitions, is enabled to preserve.

But whatever the magnitude of its failure morally and intellectually to rise to the height which the occasion demands, the Labour Movement cannot possibly be set on one side, and we must never despair of it. For that movement embodies, when all is said, three vital things. It is essentially a reply to the pretensions of plutocracy, and has grown up, as nothing else in our society has done, in order to resist them. It is, further, on the whole, a real democracy amid the shams and shadows of political forms. And, finally, it is already in a measure an engine of emancipation, capable, could it but find a true unifying principle and a programme really constructive, of forming the nucleus of a noble social order. But with all its rapid expansion in numbers and in scope, and even (in certain directions) in policy and in ideas, the Labour Movement still fails to perceive that its real task is to come to the rescue of society, and not to intervene only with the effect of dislocating it. A policy of merely frustrating capitalism will destroy the momentum of industry, without providing any unifying principle or apparatus of organization capable of bringing a "new social order" out of the chaos thus created. A true social policy for to-day would appeal to the best that was in the heart and mind of men in every stratum of society—not perhaps for identical reasons, but as tending to an identical aim. We have to ask whether either official "Labourism" or Bolshevism provides this, and if not, where else its elements are to be sought and found.

IV

We have spoken of the Labour Movement in the previous section as if the multitudinous efforts put forward by and on behalf of the working masses could be considered as part of a co-ordinated whole; but it would be difficult at a closer inspection to find those efforts united by common principles or common aims, or, indeed, by anything but a few catch-phrases expressing hostility to "capitalism." Certain broad lines of cleavage within "the ranks of Labour" are indeed clear, and becoming clearer; but there has up till recently been a tendency, in this country at any rate, to consider a few stereotyped phrases as sufficiently indicating the goal to be aimed at, and to treat the "Right," "Left," and "Centre" as if they were part of a football team, each urging forward the ball of progress by their own method when it happened to come their way. To-day Bolshevik theory and the Communist fact of Soviet Russia are rapidly dispelling this very characteristic illusion, and competing "Internationals" growl at one another with a ferocity which Socialists had generally reserved for "the master class." Despite the formation of "centre parties" for building bridges to span gulfs quite unbridgable, the main lines of division in policy and principle are clear enough; and the rank and file have to choose, if not this day, at any rate very soon, whether they will serve "official Labour" or the Communism which has its far from spiritual home in Moscow.

The choice appears for the moment inevitable, but it does not any the less present itself to us as other than a choice between two evils. Neither movement can offer us a unifying principle worthy of the name. It is true that each believes firmly enough that it possesses such a thing. "Official Labour" is a curious and obviously transitional compound of a jealously proletarian but largely defensive Trade Unionism and a theoretically "national" political party with the largest ambitions. But a formula is believed to have been found capable of developing this unwieldy structure into an impressive force. This formula is that in which Labour politicians appeal to *"workers by hand and brain"* to make alliance in the common cause of ending their servitude, and that of society, to the capitalist exploiter. The phrase is a specious one: there is, indeed, much belated commonsense in the appeal; but it may justly be doubted whether it will accomplish the miracles of social transformation which seem to be expected of it.

We need not stop to discuss the doubtful value of an implied distinction between workers by hand and by brain, for clearly no one could be an efficient worker of any sort without the use of both constantly, and often simultaneously; nor stay to inquire into which classification the skilled mechanic or the drudge on an office stool ought respectively to fall. Dangers of perpetuating social caste are not absent from the application of this formula; but its essential failure lies in its implied acceptance of capitalist criteria as to what constitutes socially valuable work. If those who challenge the economic organization of capitalism do so merely as "workers," then limitations of outlook, and even considerations of immediate self-interest, may forbid them to inquire too closely whether the particular work, on which the maintenance of their economic position appears to depend, is valid or justifiable at all from the standpoint of the general interest. Yet not until issues of this sort are fearlessly raised can the economic dominion of plutocracy be seriously shaken, and its dictation of industrial policy meet with effective reply. When the enormous scope of luxury production, the number of "parasitic" occupations, and the dissipation of human energies into channels of waste are remembered, it may be realized how many of the country's busiest "workers" would find their *immediate* economic interests seeming to lie rather with the maintenance of plutocracy than with any programme which seriously threatened to disturb it. This is, of course, particularly true of those "middle-class" hirelings of capitalist industry, for whose support official Labour is now sedulously angling. They may be gained for a *political* unification based on a common antagonism, until that opposition is faced with the prospect of effecting a constructive change which shall not damage the vested interests of any of its component parts. But once embarked on any honest effort to bring into being a "new social order," the imposing forces of Labour will melt away in acrimonious confusion. And this for the reason that no basis has been found for economic achievement or moral unity in the pursuit of a common purpose.

The force of circumstances, and an energetic propaganda, have combined during the last ten years to effect most important modifications in the complacent evolutionary collectivism which was for so long the whole social Gospel of official Labourism. But beliefs so traditional die hard, and new phraseology has not in itself gone far to create a new mentality. "Nationalization" still represents a panacea to a Labour movement with scarcely a vestige of control over "the representatives of the nation," political or bureaucratic, and therefore with scant prospect of rendering "control by the workers" effective, even if it should be nominally conceded. Vast promises are made by Labour politicians of the blessing which the workers can confidently expect will they but return them to power. But no clear recognition is shown of the fact that political methods, however necessary or valuable, are essentially passive so far as the masses are concerned, and cannot in any event do anything considerable to stimulate the initiative or prepare the democratic achievements on which alone a free society can be securely founded. Similarly, the goal of the "Leisure State" obscures the truth that such a free society is impossible unless men are consciously and positively free in the performance of their work, and not merely in their spare time. Only work done in an atmosphere of freedom can be done for its own sake, and a noble social order could not be content to apply any lesser criterion to the preponderant majority of its industrial activities. "Liberty" in the abstract is still the dream of the sentimentalists of Labour, when what they ought rather to be striving for is the achievement of definite *liberties,* through the attainment of which true liberty can alone be established—or even by the majority apprehended. But in place of this the actual struggles of the workers are far too exclusively concentrated round the issues of wages and hours, which leave them groping in a fog of materialism, and going round in circles as men do in fogs—the vicious circles to which the economic dominion of plutocracy condemns the futilities of industrial agitation.

V

Bolshevism is the nemesis of sentimental Socialism. Its theorists perceive the futility of "democracy" and "liberty," as the Labourites have been content to interpret them, and they set out to solve the problem (as it presents itself to them) of how to beat capitalism *at its own game*. That game of tyranny over personality and contempt for human will, they declare, is one that two can play, and its "bourgeois" devisers will live to meet their match in the forces of a Marx-conscious proletariat. The Bolshevik conception of the "proletariat" is its fundamental unifying principle, as is the "dictatorship" of that proletariat the uncompromising basis of its social policy. It is with these blazing torches that Bolshevism and its "third International" have aspired to kindle the fires of the World Revolution, and they have already flared wildly enough to dazzle the eyes of the wage-slaves of industrialism everywhere.

The Communist experiment which has followed on the collapse of the old social fabric in Russia—and incorporated not a few of its most evil features—has raised a storm of some of the most unscrupulous controversy (on both sides) in the history of politics. It is outside our purpose here to venture into that storm, but the political theory of the new Communism is too compelling in its challenge to be anywhere disregarded altogether.[1] We can but comment on a few of its implications and manifestations in order to support our conviction that it is not in this direction that we can look for the Idea in the strength of which society may be redeemed. Its guiding principle of "proletarianism," though the term means something very different from the mass-democracy which the innocent might imagine to be implied in it, is a conception not difficult to grasp. It involves the acceptance by a "class-conscious" and rigidly organized minority of a mission to drive society forward by every means (and without staying for a moment more of persuasion or propaganda than shall be necessary for the attainment of the required power), into a condition of life in which by the surrender of initiative to a handful of dictators, the equitable distribution of social resources can be achieved. Equality is imposed on the mass—and not discovered by them; liberty of action and expression is obliterated for opponents, and discreetly "rationed" to those who consent to the experiment; fraternity in trade union and functional association of every kind is suffered only beneath the all-pervading supervision of the omnipotent Centre.

Such being the methods of Bolshevik proletarianism, it is unnecessary to discuss how far its ultimate aims harmonize with a true ideal of social democracy, since to us it seems self-evident that no such ideal could possibly be realized by them. The desperate diseases by which the old Russian civilization was stricken may have demanded desperate remedies; but on communities from which the elements of health are not absent altogether,

[1] The social and economic tenets of Marxism, by which contemporary Communism is inspired, are closely examined in Chapter VIII of this volume.

proletarianism can act only as a poison. Applied to our own society, the conception of the "proletariat" is in every respect inadequate as a unifying principle. Many of the most essential elements, whole classes as we know them to-day, cannot be made to fit into it; or if they are so fitted, it is a violation of their legitimate character and traditions. Proletarianism involves isolation of and concentration upon the least human and truly normal of all forms of social status, with the result that the "proletariat" being taken as the centre of all, there follows a distortion of everything. The circumference of capitalist organization becomes the center of the new society. But proletarian dictatorship can never be citizen rule, nor even tend towards it; it is at best a rule in the interest of slaves, and in its working likely to operate as a more direct and concentrated rule over them. It destroys not only the idea of liberty, but the actual social autonomies within society in which men's liberties have been slowly discovered and substantiated, and without which civil liberty itself becomes a shadow.

But the vital objections to the Bolshevik principles and programme are more fundamental even than this, and do not depend upon political considerations at all. They arise from the Bolshevik claim to find in a "materialist interpretation" of the governing factors in society, past and present, a sufficient analysis of the social problem. We cannot treat here of so large a claim otherwise than by affirming a direct denial of it. Without a spiritual conception of individual destiny and social association underlying all, no movement can lead (as even Bolshevism claims that it will some day lead) to any true emancipation; for the application of such a test is the only standard and the only guarantee sufficient to establish such an achievement and to maintain it. But Bolshevism, in reaction against the illusions of a purely subjective "freedom" and a beneficent "progress," takes its stand not—as a valid theory must do—on objective rights and social will, but on objective facts and material power.

The full implications of this fundamental error have not been generally perceived, even by Bolsheviks themselves, but they are remarkable indeed. History, Art in all its branches, even the developing science of Psychology, are all subjected to the interpretations of Materialism. Marxian and neo-Marxian distortions of historical development are tolerably familiar; but it comes as something of a shock to learn from a Bolshevik *literary* critic that "the road to the conquest of the world by the proletariat is indissolubly bound up with the growth of machinery production." An almost insane glorification of the machine becomes the burden of the new "proletarian culture" which has lately arisen in Soviet Russia. The machine becomes the center of society, and its existence determines not merely the character, but even the motive of it. "The machine," says a Bolshevik critic,[1] "is not a soulless object; it is the living clot of the collective energy of workmen, which goes on living in all departments of production and serves as an inviting stimulus for the living proletariat in their further work. The machine regulates the relation of the workmen, their conduct, assigns to them definite tasks . . . in her they live. Her development is the development of the proletariat, the triumph of the machine is indissolubly bound up with the triumph of the workmen." A Bolshevik poem speaks of "a new iron blood" pouring into the workers' veins. And it is proclaimed to the world

[1] See four remarkable articles on "Proletarian Culture," by John Cournos, in *The New Europe,* vol. xiii. October-November 1919, from which the following quotations are taken.

that "the proletariat has realized that the strength of its revolution consists not alone in a political and military dictatorship, but also in a cultural dictatorship."

But Historical and Cultural Materialism are less likely to prove dangerous in their practical effect, than the attempt to discover in psychology a basis for the dictatorship of "efficiency," as judged by Marxian standards, over "the great dull and indifferent majority." In an extraordinary and very sinister article appearing recently in a British "proletarian" journal,[1] the author seeks, with an assiduity worthy of the blackest "reactionary," to find in psychological experiment a ground for the final repudiation of the very idea of democracy. "It is for the scientific Socialist to brush aside sentimental considerations," he concludes, "and plan how, in the new society *the interests of these dull people shall be safeguarded,* while at the same time their reactionary and deadening influence on creative policy, and in all matters involving a long view and the acceptance of new ideas, is eliminated." Contempt for the claims of human personality could hardly be more brutally expressed by a member of our present governing classes. If the Bolsheviks should succeed in putting down the mighty from their seats, it would only be to fill those seats again themselves. Their despotism might be benevolent, but the humble and meek would not find themselves exalted, in spirit or in station; they would remain where they are. The "sweeping away of democratic lumber," which the Bolshevik proclaims in the name of a purely intellectual revelation, would result in a "sociological Calvinism"— the rule of those "saved" by their understanding of a materialist interpretation of social phenomena over "the

[1] The *Plebs Magazine,* October 1920, "The Mechanism of the Mind," by "Nordicus."

great dull and indifferent majority." This is the new
world of Communism—a new world founded on the old
values, with fresh labels and a fresh tyranny to interpret
them.

VI

The power of the Socialist idea is undeniable. Under
its influence there has risen, perhaps, the most noble
secular movement that has succeeded in thrusting itself
through the arid soil of the modern world. But not here
can we recognize that Tree of Life, whose leaves are for
the healing of the nations. Neither "Labourism" nor
Bolshevism offers a rallying ground for those who, while
convinced of the moral impossibility and economic futility of plutocracy, are not "Progressive" nor Materialist
in their outlook. The prestige of capitalism is steadily
sinking, and its glaring inefficiency as a means of supply-
ing society with its elementary needs, spiritual and
material, is becoming more strikingly obvious as it moves
toward its perilous culmination. But men do not know
where to turn for a social principle stronger and more
attractive than that of individual "enterprise" expressing
its success by the accumulation of private gain. A doc-
trinaire rigidity of formula on the part of the opponents
of plutocracy blinds them to the essentials of that hideous philosophy, so that they are unable to perceive the
moral and practical significance of the distinction between
its normal, but venial, defects, and its desperate excesses,
which translate into virtue a sin deadly alike to those
who indulge it and those who are its victims. "Interest"
may form an unjustifiable and an ultimately intolerable
toll[1]: "profits" are the incentive and the goal of an unap-

[1] On the other hand, it is not impossible to find very valuable
social implications in the *universalising* of the dividend system.
For the views of the present writer on this subject see Chapter VII.

peasable avarice. The elimination of "profits" is an important step to the emancipation of labour, and a step that the workers might well proceed to take, if, instead of bickering with the owners of capital while remaining employed by them, they would more generally contrive means to employ capital, which would enable them to embark on responsible tasks and experiments.[1]

But though the workers' assaults on plutocracy are in many respects badly conceived and dissipated in pathetic futilities, it is not any "practical programme" merely which can wholly restore by a new inspiration the fortunes of their desperate crusade. Only the conception of Christendom, the clear vision of a society in which the free activities of men are gathered together to create a social order which can be offered as a gift to the glory of God, can achieve this. In such a society not only would the whole social order be such as man could feel to be worthy of God's purpose for mankind, but every individual in it could commend his personal activity to the Lord and Father of all, as affording him at least the opportunity to give the best that he could offer. The kingdom of God would then arise to embody—for the first time—a truly adequate conception of Vocation to its citizens, such as the mass of Christian folk, however faithful or devout, can never realize within a plutocracy, or indeed any other tyranny, communist or otherwise. The human soul would find thereby a fold to which it could at last return, and such as the most exalted ecclesiasticism could never supply while it remained within an antagonistic world order.

It is in this sense that the ideals and even the achieve-

[1] This policy has already been embraced by the guilds newly formed in building and agriculture.

ments of Mediævalism, for all their enormous imperfections, offer us a pattern so inspiring, an example so unique. We cannot, we would not if we could, "go back to the Middle Ages," but it is from the nobler efforts of the Middle Ages that we should seek to go forward, from the days before men had proved unworthy of the ideal of Christendom, and before the time when in fleeing from its corruptions they attained no new fellowship, but only "the isolation of the human soul." That ideal is one which cannot be immediately recovered: England cannot be recovered for the Faith by any wholesale "conversion." After some five centuries of "egocentric" social organization, culminating in one hundred and fifty years of plutocratic industrialism, its spiritual truths cannot be apprehended by the masses when preached to them in theological form. Nor is it easier to awaken the pious from a somnolent orthodoxy to the implications of the tremendous task to which, by their profession of their creed, they are committed. But in the process of constructing a society built as a real challenge to the existing values, an arena would be created in which the recovery of Faith would become possible, and its full meaning at last visible to the many to whom in this tangle of social apostasy it can never be revealed. The recovery of the guild, for example, would offer a glimpse of the great ideal which that indispensable organization attempted in a vital respect to fulfil. There may be few who can recognize the Rock on which Christendom must be built, but the many must set to building it, realizing gradually its full splendours as the towers rise upon their humble stones.

THE RETURN OF DOGMA

BY

HENRY H. SLESSER, Barrister-at-Law

Lecturer on Industrial Law in the University of London

Author of *The Nature of Being*, etc.

SYNOPSIS

§ 1. Dogma and Empiricism

Tendency of the age towards immediate achievement. Modern outlook fundamentally pessimistic. Destruction of freedom of personality. The true object of thought to discover Purpose. Personal certainty and dogma. Modern faith in the causal—its effect in government.

What Reality is—the world known through the Self. Solipsism, and belief in others. The belief in others a dogma. Reality to be found in creative freedom. Knowledge of event and mystical knowledge compared. The belief in the Good, Beautiful and True culminates in a belief in God as revealed by our Lord.

§ 2. Christian Dogma

The pursuit of philosophy the privilege of the few, but conduct and beauty universal interests. These involve choice. The challenge of Nietzche. The issue between Nietzche and Christianity. Sin. Ontological belief in Christ and its effects. Its sanction. The equality of man—free will. The limitations of the Stoics. Christian mysticism joyous. The Kingdom of God. Catholicism reposes upon a miraculous basis. Bergson and Will. Evolution only possible if it is creative. "Modernism" in faith self-contradictory. The philosophy of the Miraculous. The Miraculous and nomenclature. The Miraculous and art. Freedom and humour, fruits of the Miraculous. The mediæval heritage.

CHAPTER II

THE RETURN OF DOGMA

§ 1. DOGMA AND EMPIRICISM

THERE is a constant tendency in our age to be concerned with immediate achievement, rather than with ultimate object and value. We collect, analyse and arrange data of every kind; we invent and construct elaborate mechanism to constrain nature to our will; we devise innumerable schemes of social regeneration, but, generally speaking, we avoid thought as to final ends and are apt to regard them as unworthy of a modern man's consideration.

Nevertheless, it is a need of every person and of every nation, as experience is daily showing us, that effort, to be fruitful, must be based upon some fundamental assurance. Complete undogmatic agnosticism, not less than an uncritical sentimentality, result in mental and moral confusion, while, in proportion as we are inspired by certain conviction, does life become richer, art finer, and philosophy more profound.

The conclusions of modern science to which so many people now cling for guidance, even when they do attempt to give us a rule of life, are negative and dispiriting, and make it increasingly difficult for persons of sensibility to take a joyous view of life. We are told by many of our contemporaries how the world in which we live must become cold and uninhabitable, how the whole of what we cherish—our lives and institutions, both in their present form and future development—are doomed to ultimate annihilation, how, for a time, the cold-blooded reptile may survive us; but that, in the end, all our hopes and fears will find their conclusion in dissolution and endless night. The secular mortality of man is extended to everything else, and in the face of giant natural forces we are impotent. Not even the transference of interest from ourselves to our descendants can save us, for they also, we are told, are doomed to a futile destruction.

For a period we were left with a personality and will to fashion our lives for the short time allotted to us, but even in our personal small domain the naturalists now seek to enchain us. Our loves, our graces, our genius; all that makes us men, is now said to be the result of glands or of mechanical complexes which thrust us this way and that, now covering, now obtruding our subconscious self, according to the inexorable requirements of the laws of psychology. Thus we arrive at a state in which, deprived of hope, will and responsibility, man is left only with a haunting sense of his own impotence, and, with such an equipment, whose defects are but partially hidden by crude spasmodic sentimentalisms, modern reformers call upon him to renovate the world.

The normal man, however, continues to resist the subtle suggestion, repeated from so many quarters, that he is but an automaton. Regardless of authority and argument he retains a faith in his freedom and responsibility.

It has been said by Professor Bradley that the justification for philosophic inquiry is the satisfaction of curiosity, but surely the matter is deeper than that.

Every adult human being has a personal attitude towards life, more or less complete; everyone has a basis, an outlook, and a character—this is something more than mere curiousness, it is a need which is in our very nature, it is implicit in all choice and in all conduct. Everyone has a sense of what, to him, is good, beautiful and true. Even the sceptic is not doubtful of his scepticism; the pragmatist asserts as absolute truth that truth is but pragmatic. But it is the peculiar characteristic of our time that such judgments ever tend to be personal and subjective. Dogma, the universal social achievement of certainty, is almost dogmatically rejected.

It is the view of the writers of this book that in this extreme subjectivity of outlook, more particularly in the determination of the good, modern standards fail us. The transition from the merely curious speculations of the early Greeks to the vital questioning of Socrates is usually represented as a progress; if it be so, we have reverted in great measure to the earlier and more unproductive attitude.

The steadfast refusal of our empirics and relativists to enunciate and insist upon universal foundations upon which we all collectively may base our thoughts and actions is the more unfortunate because, in many ways, a great awakening is in progress amongst us. If we deplore the growth of cynicism and materialism on the one hand, we must acknowledge the reviving sense of human right on the other. Plutocracy and war flourish side by side with the emancipation of Labour and the League of Nations. Goodwill and wrong are ranged against one another more clearly than for some time past and, in the shock of their encounter, it looks as if the complacent optimism of the Victorian age could not survive. Yet, while materialism and power are fully equipped for the fight, those who hope that they are on the side of the angels lack that dogmatic unanimity of conviction which alone can spur them on to victory, and prevent the dissipation of their energies.

That bewildered attitude of the undogmatic mind, in some respects agnostic, in many superstitious, characteristic of so much of the modern outlook, is achieved by a deliberate ignoring of a vast area of human experience, namely, all that part which is not susceptible of causal demonstration; which, consequently, cannot be made the subject of scientific prediction and experiment. There is a strong tendency to believe that what cannot be weighed and assessed in terms of time and space is not real, that it is, to use the current phrase, merely subjective, and, consequently—though how the consequence arises it is difficult to see—it is of little or no importance.

Nor is this attitude merely academic; it affects all our lives, and is to be noticed even in modern legislation, more especially if the object of parliamentary benevolence be poor. A man is simple, he thinks he would live in a wooden hut; the State forbids him, thus wounding his idiosyncracy; he wishes to educate his children in the way he considers right; a curriculum which may offend the father's taste or outrage the child's temperament is thrust upon them. A workman prefers to save his money in his own way, Government prescribes the method of his insurance; he will consult a chemist as to an ailment, the law proposes to forbid. In an increasing number of ways his freedom of action is taken from him, mostly at the behest of conscientious reformers; in all matters his personal desires and choice are the last thing to be considered.

These instances may be multiplied, they are but examples of the product of the modern mentality, which tends to scout, as unworthy of consideration, all those subtle personal feelings which go to make up individuality; which are as various as the men who hold them, and, consequently, not mensurable by the political scientist.

Now Reality, so far as men can apprehend it, is largely a question of personal value. To the artist, colour is more real than sound; to the devout, grace is more immediate than circumstance; to the stockbroker, it is supposed, contangoes are more certain than plainsong; but to every man, that which is most real is in and of himself, neither the State, nor Progress, nor the Spirit of the age, nor even his psychic state, but his Soul.

Although many philosophers would once again assert the inherent independence of matter, apart from any human percipient, most people would still admit that our knowledge of the world is, at the least, considerably coloured by our personal outlook. The idealistic views of Bishop Berkeley that things are as they are perceived by the mind may have to be refined, and a sufficient distinction drawn between observed things, the observing mind and the soul; but, nevertheless, one element of truth in his doctrine remains unimpaired: that matter comes to us, whatever else it may be, as a series of events, and that, so far from objective matter being a direct experience, it is a process, partly intellectual, partly instinctive, which is derived from, and is not in itself, our original experience.

Thus, so far from the outer world being immediate and personal consciousness a secondary process; despite the new realists, it must be admitted that we still start from our consciousness and impute matter therefrom, and, if this be so, if the consciousness, if personality, be to us more real than any material world, it would appear that there is much in life which is still uncompassed by Science, for Science, and the belief in inevitable secular causation upon which it is based, can only deal with the data of experience, by comparison and experiment; the personal experience itself, and the Self must always be assumed by Science; yet, it is just this initial primordial experience which modern psychologists tend to treat as secondary and causal.

At this point the issue between the dogmatic and empirical view as revealed in the problem of Solipsism immediately arises; the problem that, if all event occurs to us only in our consciousness, it may well be that no other person exists at all except ourselves and that we are living in a dream world, peopled solely by our own imagination.

Both for empirical reasons and on dogmatic grounds deeper than those of Science, we are convinced of the reality of others. So far as regards the purely rational basis for our conviction, it may be stated thus—we know in the world of material event, that we express ourselves outwardly in certain ways; we see others do the same, consequently we ascribe to others the same operative personality which we know ourselves to possess. This is the bare justification from causation.

But this argument, like all other scientific conclusions, makes many unprovable assumptions; it assumes, first of all, the validity of cause at all as a prime influence. It may well be that what causes others to approximate to our behaviour arises from quite different origins. Next it assumes, from definable physical behavior, that elusive indescribable condition, personality. We can hardly define our own character, much less can we say how far our actions and our characters are consistent; how then can we hope to establish the personality of others from a very partial glimpse of their external behaviour? In fact it is not from any scientific induction, obtained from observation of behaviour, that we come to believe that we are not the only persons in the Universe; our real conviction arises not from a comparison of data, but as an act of faith. We believe in the reality of others because of an irresistible personal assurance that it is so. This certainty is an objective universal dogma. In sympathy and in love the assurance becomes quickened and the personalities of others become increasingly real to us; as in all true acts of faith, the dogmatic belief comes before and not after the logical demonstration. We ask of faith that it should not ignore our reason, but we are dependant for our faith on sources other than those of the rational intellect alone.

In the sense of fellowship with others, we realize our first act of faith, and, as we pass from mere recognition to sympathy, affection and love, our faith in others becomes increasingly strengthened, and all causal sociological explanation is found to be increasingly inadequate.

The implications of this fact are important; for, if there be such a thing as Progress, if man can be distinguished from the animal, if one man can be greater than another, it is just in the possession of that sympathy and love, of that spontaneous grace or talent, which science is unable to assess. Because it is spontaneous, dependant on some power quite other than any mechanistic antecedent cause, science cannot measure, classify or deal with it. The more real and deep is the possessed grace, the less is it susceptible of psychological mensuration.

It is not alone in the domain of human fellowship that dogmatic faith is more powerful than causal expectation; the whole inspiration of the artist in the cultivation of the Beautiful is similarly spontaneous and cannot be manufactured by any prescription arrived at by inductive means. Thought itself is to be valued in so far as it is both original and true. The sciences of ethics, æsthetics and logic are not creative; they catalogue, they do not make; for the foundations of science are in the determined, but the inspiration of the Good, the Beautiful and the True lie in the spontaneous and free.

It is, moreover, in the possession of creative freedom in art, learning or righteousness, that we recognize the achievement of a certainty far more real than any that can be acquired by mechanistic or logical means; so far is it from being true that the empiricist by experiment or comparative contrivance can discover Reality or a rule of life, that, in fact, an impossibility of mathematical assessment in any particular case, arising from the genius of the creative subject, is in itself some indication that Will is there enthroned and a close relation to Reality established.

We have spoken of the determined and of the spontaneous; we will define more closely the sense in which the two words are here used. The material world, which common sense and Science seek to explain, consists in the first place of a series of events, each event in a sense unique, but so far resembling another, that a common noun such as "table," or "chair," can be employed to describe their common properties, which name is indeed a prophecy that what the objects named have been found to do in the past, under certain circumstances, they will again do in the future. Thus the word "sun" is inseparably connected with its daily appearance over the horizon, but the use of the word need not blind us to the fact that, so far as we know, there is no inherent reason why the sun should rise to-morrow morning. The word "sun" certainly gives us such an expectation, but the sun as an event may always come to disappoint it.

Thus the whole structure upon which the modern empirical position rests, the notion of inevitable and uniform causation, is based upon the assumption, which language tacitly assumes as a basis for nomenclature, that what has happened before will happen again, and in no sense can logic or common sense claim any certainty greater than this contingent or logical one.

Contrast this with the certainty of the spontaneous, which Personality with all its fruits, produces. Here Activity, not Repetition, is the principal characteristic; in no sense can genius or even character be predicted, and it is, as we have seen, only the lower and fundamentally less real parts of man's nature which can be the subject of prediction or of adequate definition at all since they alone display the comparative monotony of repetition.

It may be urged by some that because Science is as yet incompetent to compass the higher reaches of our nature, this arises from a deficiency of knowledge and in no sense proves the non-mechanical nature of personality. It is true that the mere limitations of present science do not of themselves prove the reality of personal Will, but, when it is remembered that personality and Will are themselves outside the Time-Space process which science assumes; in which science and verbal terminology function; and that the individual person only uses these forms for the purpose of comprehending event, it will be recognized that the spontaneous, which is in the true sense of the word infinite in character, cannot be the creature of mechanism, itself a finite compound.

If this be true, it is not a failure in degree, but in kind, which prevents Science and language from adequately describing personality, nor can any extension of a method based upon repetition come any nearer to the comprehension of that which is free, timeless, without space, and, in the ordinary modern acceptation of the word, without Cause.

A Being of Will such as the human soul, if it is to have any supreme guidance, must therefore seeks its inspiration, more particularly in its personal creative acts, in some assured fundament other than that which derives from mere knowledge of past or prediction of future event. An expediency based upon experience, sagacity or any other fundament which is causal or empirical in origin, must fail the free spirit.

We would prefer to claim, as a basis for our assurance, a dogmatic belief in the supremacy of the Good, the True and Beautiful, which must almost necessarily lead us to the belief in the supremacy of God, in Whom these three certainties find their culmination, and, if the revelation of God by our Lord is the incarnation of the highest norm we can conceive, it is in Him that we shall presently discover our ultimate certainty and standard.

It is said of the Tichborne claimant that, on his examination, he translated the words "Laus Deo" as the "Laws of God." In a sense he was speaking more truly than he knew, for, in a sufficient praise and appreciation of the divine law we may obtain our deepest insight into Reality.

§ 2. CHRISTIAN DOGMA

The study of truth pursued in philosophy and logic may be the privilege of the few, but to all men is given, in some measure, a dogmatic understanding of the difference between right and wrong, between beauty and ugliness.

Bernard Shaw, in his play "Major Barbara," is scornful of those who, having no knowledge or art or philos-

ophy, are yet ready to make moral judgments; yet, in
this, as in so many other matters, Shaw is but quarrelling
with what is a patent truth of human nature. A child
will appreciate the difference between being good and
naughty, will enjoy beauty, long before he will learn to
reason, and it is natural that he should do so, for, avoid
it as we may, it is a fact which no difference or scepticism
can obscure, that the pursuit of goodness and beauty are
the fundamental concerns of man.

Of late years we have seen a most courageous and
unqualified attack upon the Christian rule of life led by
Nietzche; that master of phrase and denunciation. This
attack has once more made clear, by antithesis, the extraordinary claim and grandeur of the Christian ideal.
Broadly speaking, the issue between Christianity and the
Nietzchean creed is that the one is in essence paradoxical,
in that it is contrary to our animal nature, whereas the
other exalts the so-called natural law into a religion.
That power, pride and circumstance are fundamental
goods, is affirmed by the Nietzchean and denied by the
Christian ethic, and between these two lie all those com-
promises and qualifications which distinguish religious
and ethical systems in general.

There is in every being a desire to achieve survival, a
desire which shows itself not only in humanity but in all
nature, and this desire to survive at any cost readily
develops in man into an appetite to acquire dominion of
one kind or another for selfish ends over others, and it is
this desire for dominion, which is inherent in greater or
less degree in all men, which is fairly and dogmatically
called by the theologians a sin.

The teaching of our Lord is a repudiation of this sin
of dominion, which repudiation shows itself in many
respects, ranging from martyrdom, the abandonment of

the natural wish for earthly survival, to courtesy, the voluntary abstention from over self-assertion. It is moreover unique, in that, although the notion of triumph over animal nature is adumbrated among the Greek and Chinese moralists and finds expression in the teachings of Aknahton of Egypt, the paradoxical completeness of the teaching, together with an ungrudging recognition of the divine personality of the teacher, are only to be found in that one instance of the faith which was, until recently, a dogmatic conviction for many millions of educated and uneducated persons.

Whether this ontological faith in the complete and real divinity of Christ be justified or not, it must be admitted that its presence yields an entirely different quality to belief, whether for better or for worse, than arises from a bare acceptance of the morality in itself or from a qualifying arianism such as is taught by many humanitarians. The jurist Austin has shown us how, behind every operative obligation, there lies some sanction, punitive, retributive or other; and the absence of sanction, it is believed, must in the end tend to emasculate faith, and render it impotent to fight against the allurements of power and unrestrained ambition.

The mystical assertion of the equality of all men before God, inherent in the Catholic faith, which is the negation of the worth of secular dominion, assumes every man to be capable of moral freedom, and assumes, moreover, that the value of every man's judgment lies in his sacred personality; in his possession of a soul, and not in any extrinsic material circumstances of race, rank or fortune.

The Catholic must believe that the gift of that personality is certainly not a matter to be predicted in mechanical terms; the movements of the Holy Spirit lie clean outside

Science and Psychology, for the Spirit is directly associated with the Personality, which is therefore itself a reality having no antecedent human cause.

Thus, we are brought to the dogmatic belief again, through the observation of man's moral life, that the freedom of the soul, which is the liberty of God, is the basis of the whole human spiritual world, and that, so far from the deepest things of life being material, the free soul is operated by the influence of the Holy Spirit and is, even in its relative life on earth, itself spontaneous and immortal.

It is curious and typical of the present confusion of mind, that the modern sceptical materialist should so often proclaim himself a democrat, for, if the mystical dogma of equality and grace and its corollary of freedom be rejected, and man be conceived as the creature of circumstance, there would appear to be a thousand reasons why, as a result of breeding, education and selection, men of varying degrees of value might be produced. In this connection perhaps it is strange to notice that Plato, the father of Idealism in metaphysic, very illogically accepts the whole deterministic position, when, in his Republic, he calls for aristocracy and the special breeding of men.

It is essential, however, in these matters, that we should do justice to the Stoical position. The Stoics, like the Christians, asserted the universality of man, his inherent equality and right to equal treatment. And if, therefore, we come to the conclusion that it is only either in the egalitarianism of the Stoic or the Catholic that the highest morality is to be found, we have yet to show why it is that, in this respect, Stoicism fails us and Catholicism is adequate.

The difficulty which was ever present to the Stoic mind

was that the system of universal justice for which he contended lacked any dogmatic or compelling basis. In vain did he invoke that curious abstraction, "The Law of Nature," as a justification for what must seem to every unprejudiced person a rule of life wholly paradoxical; contrary to the order of nature which he invoked; contrary to the policy of the Roman Empire in which he acquiesced; and contrary to the immediate interests of the individual to whom he preached. There arises, in consequence, among the Stoics, as among many modern humanitarians, a somewhat sententious solemnity and joylessness of outlook; indeed a fundamental pessimism, against which the Epicureans very naturally protested and of which the Cynics made a mock. The truth is that, in the paradoxical implications of Stoicism and Catholicism alike, the demands for service made by those doctrines can only be sustained through a very vivid and personal dogmatic mysticism and, that such mysticism may be in harmony with man's nature, it must needs be a mysticism of a very joyous kind.

We find in the moral sphere that a vast change of outlook, absent in pagan sagacity, is proclaimed by that great dogmatic ordinance which may be best summarized in the command "Return good for evil." It cannot be over-emphasized how entirely revolutionary, and, in the sense in which the word has been used, paradoxical, is this precept; as indeed, is the whole doctrine of the Sermon on the Mount, enjoining man not to seek his highest good in his own preservation, nor in wisdom, caution, temperance, or even justice, as do the philosophers, but in boldly claiming from him an entire subversion of his lower nature, the repudiation of selfishness and a recognition of his duty as a co-operative builder of God's kingdom.

The scope and implications of the Catholic creed will be discussed in this book by others more competent to deal with the subject; for the moment I am only concerned to show that not only do we need dogma for right living, but that the miraculous dogmas of the Catholic Church are the ones which we should accept.

It is not denied for a moment that the Catholic faith rests upon a miraculous basis, but, even if we approach the problem of Being from the narrower standpoint of Science; it would appear that, in the last resort, we shall have to invoke the notion of spontaneous Will, akin to the miraculous, to account for the development of organisms, if not also for their mere continuity. Thus Bergson points out very clearly, in his *Creative Evolution,* that variation and change can only occur in an organism through the introduction of new unaccountable elements, and it would appear, when the matter is closely considered, that the whole notion of development is otherwise self-contradictory, in that, if the tendencies to change are only innate in the beginning, they cannot be the cause alone, without an external influence, of their own actualization; while, if the change is overt from the outset, it was strictly present from the beginning of the transition and there was really no new element of change developed at all.

Nevertheless, while tardily admitting the volitional element in life, the full significance of the spontaneous and unassessable elements in creation are apt to be scouted even by the most modern psychologists who continue to apply to the divine characteristics of man, methods which may be suited to the study of molecules in in a laboratory.[1] When, however, we do unreservedly

[1] The work of Dr. Berman, *The Glands Affecting Personality,* is very typical of this modern mentality. In it appears the following

bring ourselves fully to appreciate the working of Will in man, it becomes evident that the essential value of high morality and art in men and nations is that it frees them from those mechanical causal habits which are called, somewhat unfairly animal, for the free pursuit by a free personality of the Good, the Beautiful and the True. We believe, as a dogma, that all mankind are capable of this emancipation, and there is considerable desire to admit possibilities of redemption to the animal kingdom generally, if not to the whole Universe.

With this view of a miraculous created world before us, it may appear extraordinary to many, who are not Christians at all, that modernists should so fear dogma that they should be at pains to modernize and explain away that miraculous basis of life on which not only Christianity, but all art and even all joyous living depend.

Dr. Weston, the Bishop of Zanzibar, points out that, even in the Roman Church, modernization and the "symbolical reading" of the things defined by the Vatican Councils and the Early Fathers is in rapid progress,[1] and the tendency to surrender to the spirit of the age in hypostatizing causation is not confined to any particular Church.

Despite the apologetics of modernists, it cannot be too clearly recognized by Catholics, as in deed it is assumed by their sceptical opponents, that Christianity is, emphatically, a religion which involves in its very nature a full and adequate dogmatic recognition of the miraculous.

passage: "The distinction between men of theoretical genius whose minds could embrace a universe, and yet fail to manage successfully their own personal lives, and the men of practical genius who can achieve and execute . . . lies primarily in the balance between the ante-pituitary and the adrenal cortex. Men like Abraham Lincoln and George Bernard Shaw belong to this ante-pituitary group."

[1] *The Christ and His Critics*, chapter i.

However the idea of miracle may be distorted in popular debate, it is idle to deny that Christianity, so far from asserting the rigid uniformity of fate and so-called "natural" law, is a standing qualification of it and refutation of its universality.

In the moral field, the automatic struggle for existence, dear to the evolutionist, is supplanted by the paradoxical ideals of Mercy and Love—in the material world, the fatalistic notions of heredity and environment are contradicted in the belief in Personality, in social and individual Grace.

If, then, the miraculous be that which has no secular antecedent cause, at any rate no finite calculable one—Christianity, so far from denying that effects may be produced immediately by the Holy Spirit, asserts that this miracle is not only a common experience but that such inexplicable ultra-material intervention, is essentially true Reality.

It is, nevertheless, right, despite the subordination of the causal to the miraculous, that we should not fall into the error of the Manichæans and despise the material, but that we should study and endeavour to understand the arena in which our will contends, in which, as in all creation, we assert that the universal Will is immanent.

We have seen how our whole causal life and all science and nomenclature rest upon the expectation of repetition. A noun, the name of a thing, is a prophecy of what the thing will do in a certain event. If we call a certain phenomenon "wood," it is because we impute to it a certain essential quality, say inflammability, and, in so doing, predict that under certain circumstances it will burn. This is the case with all those common nouns descriptive of things as events with which we are primarily concerned in discussing the miraculous.

A statement, concerning an event, must, however, contain a verb, to describe the thing achieving its potentialities as well as a noun, and it is when this verb contains descriptions of events, the possibility of which is inconsistent, or thought to be inconsistent, with the essence of the subject noun that the question of a miracle arises. We do not normally impute to water the quality of becoming wine. If, therefore, water change into wine, our terminological basis, in the narrow sense, undoubtedly tends to fail us.

Reliance on inevitable repetition as a universal rule of life and our logical apparatus are therefore both obstacles to a reception of the miraculous; but, seeing that, in fact, the spontaneous, which we have recognized in Will, is the negation of repetition and yet must be admitted into our experience; it would seem that our logical equipment, which is so largely based upon the assumption of natural uniformity, is inadequate to compass our whole knowledge.

In all metaphysic this is, in a sense, assumed—Philosophy, like all other verbal communication, consists of statements; in every metaphysical assertion there is a subject and a predicate, but, unlike the case of Science, in Philosophy, as in religion, the subject-matter to be explained must contain all experience, and, unless the predicate exceeds such rational experience, the belief as to the ultimates of knowledge must remain merely sceptical.

Thus, finally, we are driven to notions, which, by reason of their non-causal and non-repetitive nature, we cannot render in complete predication. Yet we have seen that it is just in the affirmation of the miraculous, where our logical equipment is inadequate, that we touch Reality. It is no objection to our employment of words or arts to symbolize the real that we cannot furnish them with a complete connotation, the deficiency lies in our own mentality and not in the notion; we may continue to use arts and faith which embody the miraculous with confidence—the dogmatic belief in God, the divinity of our Lord, and other sublime notions are not the less real to us because we cannot give to them a definition based upon common repetitive Aristotelian logic.

Neither of the objections to the miraculous therefore; neither the dogmatic assertion of a fated repetition which is avoided in the reality of experience, nor the objection of a repetitive logic are sound; the former is not only unsound but untrue to our experience; the latter, with its insistence upon essence and accident, on noun and verb, is based upon the causal notion of universal repetition, and in the last resort, stands and falls with that assumption. It is, indeed, only in a world exclusively governed by rigid fate, that the Aristotelian distinction of essence and contradiction, in noun and verb, can be maintained.

Directly the free spontaneous intervenes, as in the operations of personality, love, beauty or grace, the exclusive logical causal, based upon an assumption of repetition, fails us; it is interesting to observe that it is just at this time that the artist and the devout supplant the scientist and logician.

All true art, like all true faith, must recognize the miraculous; the sciences of æsthetics and ethics have proved their total incapacity, owing to their causal and comparative method, to deal with that which surpasses the dogma of repetition.

To summarize, we have experience of two worlds: the one to which the modern sceptics have exclusively pinned their faith, the repetitive, causal and uninspired, the world of appearance; and the other, the real world, the

experience of which is far more poignant and immediate,
the world of the miracle and the spirit, the creative
original state which we recognize in creative art.   No
noun of generalization can hope to symbolize it adequately; the approach to the understanding of it is
primarily through the certainties of inspiration and
through art and grace.

Not the least of the endowments of the belief in
essential freedom is the gift of Comedy.   Bergson, in his
essay on Laughter, has pointed out how the sense of
comic is founded upon the unexpected.   From humour to
joy is an easy step, and from joy to consolation.   It is to
be observed how those caricatures of Christianity which
are based upon the mechanistic unchristian view of predestination unfailingly produce their share of the solemn,
the gloomy and the pretentious.   It is not the least-con-
siderable advantage of spiritual freedom that it keeps us
sweet.

Enough has been said to show that it is in the spontaneous miraculous and not in any mechanical system that
the highest life consists.   A Christian may therefore
approach the miraculous basis upon which his creed
reposes with a very real feeling that, whatever else may
be revealed by it, the fact that it is miraculous, so far
from being any argument against its validity, is in itself
an earnest and an essential part of the belief.

There have been men who have sought for a Beethoven
in terms of climate, race, or possibly of phosphates; but
the common sense of the ordinary man and the intuition
of the imaginative will continue to regard genius as a
miracle.   If then man, heightened by genius, can produce
great artistic results by no material agency: how much
more likely is it that the Divine Will, which inspires even
that human one which we find in genius, can itself, on its

own occasion, produce miraculous changes in the order of nature?

The miraculous is seen to show itself in two forms at least. There are cases where the order of nature has been, and continues to be, superseded; cases where we should expect to find spontaneous Will still enmeshed in causal Substance; and these miracles we believe to be only possible to the Author of Will and Substance alike, or possibly to those receiving directly delegated powers. But, over and beyond this, there remains the whole gamut of the miraculous; varying from so detached and vital a case as the conversion of St. Paul to the inspiration of the artist and the smallest liberation from necessity achieved by any creature.

We have seen that, in the last resort, what is most important in life cannot be defined by reason or adequately named in words, nevertheless, it is a necessity of our nature to endeavour to obtain some certain postulate as a guidance in affairs which we can all share. All men have to act, and all conduct which is at all social must rest upon a dogma. The true question for us is not one as between doubt and certitude; for all conduct rests ultimately upon temporary certainty, but it is a choice between one continuing sufficient dogma and a series of inconsistent experiments in faith.

The last decade has been one of anarchy in ideal and practice. Revolt as a good in itself: theosophy, Christian Science, patriotism, pacifism, magic, spiritualism, psychocomplexities and autosuggestions, beliefs in majorities, and, later, in minorities; all these have in turn been offered to a bewildered people struggling to the light. Against these ephemeral doctrines we offer the old yet ever-living dogma of the Catholic Faith as a balm and corrective to our present discontents.

We recognize in the world an increasing desire for a dogmatic basis of life; we realize the slow but growing conviction that, in essentials, the faithful of the Middle Ages, despite their failures in practice, possessed a rule of life and a sense of beauty which we are painfully endeavouring to recover. We are not ashamed to preach those old doctrines from which many have turned as too superstitious for their use. What these doctrines are and what their moral, social and economic implications, those who come after me have endeavoured to explain.

THE NECESSITY OF CATHOLIC DOGMA

BY

Fr. L. S. THORNTON, M.A.

Priest of the Community of the Resurrection, Mirfield
Author of *Conduct and the Supernatural*

SYNOPSIS

1. THE FAILURE OF MODERN CIVILIZATION.

> Due to its being unlike the Kingdom of God.
> Its characteristics: secularism, individualism, mechanism.
> Its bankruptcy and need of redemption.
> The return of Catholicism.

2. REDEMPTIVE VALUE OF THE CREED.

> Catholic dogma the key. Return to God.
> *Catholic doctrine of God* the necessary ground of society.
> The redemptive action of God makes possible a hope of renovation.
> Social significance of the Creed.
> *The Gospel miracles* give a revelation of values.
> They assert the reality of God's freedom.
> They declare redemption to be a divine work which man needs because he cannot reform himself.
> *The Creed* discloses the meaning of personality in God and in man.
> Divine Love.
> The value of human personality.

3. REDEEMED SOCIETY.

> Redemption is already a fact.
> A new social order appeared in the early Church.
> It can only be explained by reference to *an experience of redemption.*
> This experience requires a theological explanation and involves dogmatic statements.
> The experience of divine grace inspires hope of social transformation.
> *The Holy Spirit* transforms personal relationships from within. The power of the Cross. The indwelling of Christ Crucified.
> *The Resurrection of the Body* gives value to the whole material order.
> *The Sacraments* emphasize the unity of soul and body, religion and the social order. Worship and work. The Eucharist as symbol of Christendom.

CHAPTER III

THE NECESSITY OF CATHOLIC DOGMA

PREVIOUS essays have indicated that Society must be reintegrated upon a dogmatic basis, and that the common end which men must set before themselves is the Christian ideal of the Kingdom of God. Such a reintegration would be "Christendom," an international world-order bound together in a common allegiance to Christ strong enough to transcend all barriers. Such a Christendom would possess its own many-sided culture penetrating all grades of society; and the whole would be held together by a great common tradition of religious experience in which each individual has an intimate share. It is a fundamental belief of those who contribute to the present work that the ancient dogmas of Catholicism provide the only adequate basis upon which a restored Christendom can be built.

I

The precarious condition to which modern civilization has been reduced is due to the inadequate foundations upon which it has been built. For it took its rise in reaction from an intensely theocratic conception of society held in the Middle Ages, and in consequence of its initial bias it has always tended to represent in a one-sided way a quite opposite group of tendencies. Whatever we may think of particular embodiments of the Kingdom of God in the past, it is becoming increasingly certain that the failure of modern civilization is due to its unlikeness in almost every respect to any form of society which the idea of the Kingdom of God could possibly suggest. For the root idea of the Kingdom of God is that human society does not exist either by its own right, or for its own ends, but that it has a Divine Ruler to whom it belongs, Who founded it by His creative power, and Who impressed His divine will upon its constitution. Dependence is thus the aspect of human nature which is emphasized in this doctrine of the Kingdom. Man owes his origin to the divine will, and for the realization of his destiny he depends upon a wide all-embracing purpose conceived in the divine mind. Society, grounded upon God, has thus an ideal necessary unity of its own, and a common end towards which it must move. And with this common recognition of God as the ground of human life goes a mutual dependence of men upon one another. Men are not at liberty to do as they like; for they exist as parts of a larger social whole which sets a limit to their freedom because it is itself the divinely appointed environment of their life. A civilization which was deliberately framed in conformity to this conception of the Kingdom of God would necessarily have religion for its central bond. The idea of God would be determinative for all other ideas round which such a civilization was built. All the relationships existing in society would be subordinated to a moral ideal, the source of which would be found in the character of God Himself. Religion would inform all human activities, inspiring some, controlling and purifying others, giving a divine reference to all things human by persuading men that their highest achievements could only spring from faith and the spirit of consecration in a life of mutual service.

With such ideas as these, however, the root principles of our present civilization have scarely anything in common. Modern society took its rise from an age of humanism and individualism; and it has borne those marks upon it ever since, only developing them to their logical conclusions. On its religious side it has steadily pushed God away into as remote a position as possible. Its typical theological systems made Him an inscrutable autocrat, who cares for a few favoured persons and rejects the vast majority of mankind. It has thus secularized one department of life after another, and divorced them from all connection with religion. It has torn God from the centre and placed Him on the circumference. In His place it has put man as the measure of all things. Along with this dethronement of God has gone the doctrine of individualism, one of the cornerstones of the modern world. In place of the older doctrine of the mutual dependence of persons in a common dependence upon God, came another idea of solitary self-centred personality, which first of all made religion a private affair, and so obtained religious sanction for the belief that everything else ought to be given the same private and self-centred form. The new point of view spread itself over every sphere, theoretical and practical alike. The individual was conceived as a self-sufficient unit, born free and inheriting absolute rights and liberties. Freedom in a secularized and individualistic world is bound to be interpreted in an irresponsible sense, consequently this irresponsible doctrine of liberty is in the end seen to involve the destruction of all liberties. What seems to give more scope to the individual eventually brings all men under bondage to necessity by making the selfishness of the few to be the law of life for the many. Thus we are expected to submit to economic laws which are in reality simply the permanent tendencies of self-interest dressed up in solemn legal garb. It follows that justice is replaced by sophistry because the sacred ark of egoism must not be touched. To such depths of fatuity will men sink in their veneration for selfish superstitions. But where justice is destroyed, society must break up. The same must be said of truth. The philosophers turned the doctrine of liberty to yet another use by making the pursuit of truth a private affair of personal introspection. Here also the self-sufficiency of man was implicitly trusted.

This world of individualism was naturally a materialistic mechanical world. Where there is no ideal of fellowship, individualism must needs find for itself a more artificial and automatic system of supports, which will not demand the arduous exercise of social activity. During the past century men had been led to suppose that they had secured such a system in a world of highly elaborated mechanical contrivances which provided a temporary basis of material prosperity. As long as this imposing external exhibition continued it was naturally interpreted as a sign that a high level of culture had been attained. On the other hand, the collapse of this artificial world of mechanism reveals strikingly the actual impotence of modern man. The real liberty which is only achieved through recognition of the mutual dependence of persons in society has been at a discount all the time. In such a time of disillusionment there is real danger that men will cease to believe in liberty.

Meanwhile there are signs at least that the folly of some of these doctrines is being understood. Recent psychology lays emphasis upon the social aspects of the individual and the necessity of co-operation. The individual, we are told, does not possess liberty naturally, but must achieve it by severe social effort.[1] Yet the mere discovery of truer social theories will not carry us far. The creative energy, loyalty, and self-sacrifice which such theories demand lie far above the level which the average man is capable of attaining. The old mythology of natural goodness and inevitable progress has been exposed. We cannot assume any inevitable process which will enable men to attain a common mind and will. The only thing which appears inevitable, humanly speaking, is a perpetual conflict of interests ending in catastrophe.

Indeed, Professor Royce pointed out before the war that the problem of the individual becomes more and more acute as civilization develops. "The diseases of self-consciousness are due to the inmost nature of our social race. . . .They increase with cultivation."[2] What Royce asserted of the individual is equally true of the nation and of other self-centred groups. The pressing logic of facts is making it clearer every day that there are disruptive tendencies in human nature, which are a permanent danger to society. That fundamental self-assertion of the individual and his interests, which is known to theology as "original sin," is not less prominent to-day than in the past, and there is not the smallest ground on any analysis of natural human resources for supposing that it will ever be anything else.

It is this situation which calls loudly for a return of Catholic Christendom. Protestantism is helpless; for its distortion of both religion and morality is largely responsible for the actual state of things. It destroyed the only world-wide fellowship man has ever known, and broke up that unity of belief upon which it rested. Now there hardly exists any common tradition of belief in respect of

[1] M. P. Follett, *The New State.*
[2] Royce, *Problem of Christianity*, vol i. pp. 156, 157.

either truth or justice regarded as objective spiritual goods. Reason divorced from faith becomes destructive of the one, whilst blind self-interest makes the other seem impossible.

Thus on every side we see no hope for the future of society, unless it can be redeemed from its miseries by some power beyond itself; which can, not only exorcise the demons of proud self-complacency, selfish greed, materialism and black despair which alternately fill it, but also build it afresh on altogether new foundations. To this situation Catholicism has its answer. Only God can redeem, as He alone can create; and there is no remedy for these maladies except that which the Catholic Gospel provides. The misery and confusion of our modern world and the incapacity of all its boasted knowledge to find any way out—all these things are so many signs pointing us back to the old foundations.

II

The world evidently needs salvation, and it can only be saved by returning once more to a belief in God. Yet not any doctrine about God will do. The solitary far-off God of Unitarian deism cannot help us; for it is that kind of belief more than any other, perhaps, which has robbed the world of its religious significance and left man alone to the slavery of self-interest. Neither will the various pantheistic systems be of any use; for they offer no help from beyond this world, and it is precisely this world which needs deliverance. Nor, again, can we turn to a limited God, however much goodwill he may be supposed to possess. A God who is to save the world must be one who already controls and rules it, its Author and Creator, who stands above its weakness and confusion, and presides over its destinies with sovereign authority. Yet He must be also One who comes to the rescue of the world and acts with power and purpose, and sympathetic understanding for its needs. Such is the God whose self-revelation is recorded in the Scriptures, and whose Name comes to us through the age-long Christian tradition. It comes to us in a doctrine embodying an immense range of religious experience which was the accepted foundation of Christendom for centuries; whilst the records of its first appearance in history bear unmistakable marks of a divine revelation.

When European civilization was consciously built upon this dogma it believed also of necessity in a common ideal of justice and fellowship for man. The one was a consequence of the other. And if we go back to the origins of the doctrine in the Bible, we find that it was the unveiling of God's character and being which was the foundation of the whole conception of a Kingdom of God. In the minds of the prophets the two ideas were inseparable. As the reality and holiness of God were borne in upon their minds, so the vision of a kingdom of righteousness on earth inevitably followed. And when revelation reached a more intimate stage, and God condescended to appear on earth in human form and disclose His inmost life as a fellowship of personal relationships, Father, Son, and Holy Spirit, then a corresponding advance in man's social ideal appeared. A new embodiment of the Kingdom of God was realized in the Apostolic Church, in which not merely justice but a universal all-embracing love became the accepted law of life.

But human society needs not only a revelation of God's nature and character to furnish the ground and standard of its life. It needs above all things a power from God to enable it to live according to the ideal which is thus dis-

closed. It needs not only revelation, but redemption.
Here, again, there is no redemption adequate to its need,
save that which is offered by Catholic dogma. God has
revealed Himself by His acts in history. He chose a
people and trained them to the knowledge of Himself.
He preserved a remnant of them through centuries of
changing fortune, and kept alive in them the conviction
that through their agency His Kingdom would finally be
established. Then, since the whole human race whom
He created had wandered from the right path into a hopeless and helpless state of sinfulness, God intervened in
the course of nature for its redemption. Nature had
failed; nothing could help it but a new creative act of
God, or rather a series of acts unmistakably supernatural
in character. So the Son of God became Man and was
born of a Virgin, worked miracles upon earth, lived and
died and rose from the dead, taking again His body and
ascending into heaven. So, too, on the basis of these
redemptive acts He instituted the Catholic Church, pouring His Spirit into it and so creating in it a new centre
of world-wide fellowship.

Now, if these events really happened, as we firmly
believe, then every one of them is charged with a moral
and social significance of the most overwhelming kind.
The Catholic Creed has suffered too long from being
treated either simply as a badge of orthodoxy, a piece of
defensive armour against erroneous beliefs, or as a summary of remote events in history which have indeed sentimental associations for believers, but little or no connection with the problems of our common life in society.
The Gospel was not so regarded by the early Christians.
It was a sword which cut them off from pagan society and
dispatched martyrs to their death; a golden bond which
bound men together in unworldly fellowship; a moral

dynamic which turned the world upside down. To many people the present capitalist degradation of society seems to embody inevitable laws which cannot be altered. In a mechanical world everything encourages men to believe that they are governed by a fate which leaves no room for freedom either in God or man. The miraculous events of the Gospel are a declaration that this view is false. They declare that God is free, that so far from being a slave to nature's necessities He is able to subordinate them to His own purposes. The difficulty which men have in appreciating this idea to-day is only part of a general difficulty of the imagination which, in an artificial machine-made civilization, makes any really creative act seem impossible. But, when once this characteristic is acknowledged to be one of the marks of spiritual bankruptcy in modern life, the assertion of divine freedom in miraculous events is seen to be not only rational, but necessary if man's need is to be met effectually. The miracles of the Gospel are thus symbols of the reality of God's Personality to a world which has largely ceased to believe in personal values.

But, secondly, the Gospel miracles also characterize the nature of the redemption which man needs. In the optimistic days of the nineteenth century, when people of all views believed in an inevitable progress to a social millennium by the method of social reform, a humanitarian type of religion was put forward and became widely accepted because it so entirely harmonized with this point of view. According to it the Christian religion consisted in believing that God is our Father, and that all men are brothers; that Christ was a good Man who taught this, and enforced it by His example. In short, that He came not to redeem society, but to teach men how to reform society. And there are still plenty of people who think that

"Christianity" as they call it is "useful to society," that it is a sort of medicine to be taken in modest doses to keep the social sickness from becoming too obvious, that it is to do the ambulance work, to encourage men in patching up an old world. If the Gospel is really only a modest programme of social reform for a world which can save itself, then, indeed, miracles are out of place, and there was no need for the Son of God to become Incarnate. But this point of view is out of date. A bankrupt world needs the assurance that it is redeemed by God in spite of itself. The miracles of the Gospel declare that redemption is an act of God from first to last. Man can only desire it, yearn for it, and accept it gratefully and humbly when it is given. Yet here, again, though it is God's act, it is not inevitable. The free act of God does not treat man as a puppet, but rather makes possible his free response. Thus the Son of God was born of a Virgin to assure us that the New Creation was God's act, and not man's; yet the miracle could not take place until Mary had freely accepted the Divine gift, acting as sponsor for us all in this.

Once more, the method of redemption is intensely personal. It declares not only the reality of God's Personality, but the inmost meaning and significance of personality in both God and man. God is declared to be One whose greatness and power is manifested in loving condescension which stoops to the dust, humbles itself to the lowest level, and stops at nothing to achieve its purpose. God identifies Himself with the common experience of human life; accepts its drudgery and becomes intimate with the sordidness of sinful man; submits to maltreatment at his hands, and suffers Himself to be tested to the uttermost in torture and death. And the same life which gave a personal revelation of Divine Love also created a new idea of the meaning and worth of human personality. To our modern world which exalts mechanism and fate, and despises the worth of free personal life, for all its catchwords of liberty, to such a world the Life and Death of Christ declare the dignity of human nature and the worth of personality in man. If God Incarnate lived as a poor man and worked in a carpenter's shop, and if the Manhood in which He did these things suffered death for all and is now on the throne of heaven; then it is a blasphemous insult to that Manhood to treat any man's liberty as an indifferent thing on grounds of class or colour. If the Son of God took the nature which is common to us all, and by so doing declared the spiritual dignity of every human being, then the present social order is an open denial of Christ; for it condemns the majority of mankind to be economic slaves ministering to the selfishness of the minority. To acquiese in it is to crucify Christ afresh. According to His own declaration Our Lord came to give His Life as a ransom—that is to redeem men from slavery; "to proclaim release to the captives, to set at liberty them that are bruised." We cannot set any *a priori* limit to this Gospel of emancipation, such as, for example, is to be found in the strange idea that it is confined to the salvation of the soul from personal sin, and is irrespective of bodily and social conditions, however inconsistent these may be with the true dignity of human personality.

III

It is of vital importance to human society that it should accept the revelation of personal values, divine and human, involved in the historic facts of the Creed. But it is still more important to realize that the work of man's redemption was actually accomplished through those events; and to understand in what way the power of this redemptive work is actually available to-day for the renovation of our common life.

The Gospel of Christ was essentially one of re-creation. It not only set up a new social ideal. It actually inaugurated a new society, founded by the creative act of God, and built upon His redemptive work. It is a plain historical fact that in the first days of the early apostolic Church a new social order has already appeared. Personal relationships are on a new footing, extending even to communal possession of property.[1] In this community the relation of the individual to society has already been solved. The ideal of brotherly love is seen in action, successfully realized as a growing vital thing extending itself rapidly from place to place. The new movement produces also an immensely rich moral literature, containing an altogether new set of ideals which are applied to every form of social relationship. The unit of this new society is depicted as a new type of character, unheard of in the world before, and actually realized in a pre-eminent degree. The sociological significance of the Gospel declared itself at once in its power to produce a unique kind of life manifested in a new social order. Here we see in germ the whole possibility of Christendom, a realized Kingdom of God on earth. The form which this idea has already taken in history is discussed elsewhere in this book. We are here only concerned with the connection between this new social order and the dogmas and facts of the Catholic Creed. That there *is* a vital connection is the universal conviction of the New Testament writers, and of all orthodox Christian theology since, representing a continuous and overwhelming weight of religious experience of every age. The new

[1] Acts ii. and iv.

community, as soon as it appeared and continuously ever since, has traced it origin to an act of God. It is what it is because it is the redeemed community. Its common life is traced to a common salvation. Its members find their universal bond of fellowship in loyalty to the Lord who died for their redemption. This fellowship was created and is sustained by the indwelling presence of the Holy Spirit who conveys to all a new life from God—the power and efficacy of Christ's life and death and resurrection. We cannot enter here into the wide fields of theological speculation and definition which have arisen out of these central facts of Christian experience. Nor is it necessary to the present argument. It is sufficient to observe that the whole social structure of Christendom, as it has appeared in history, must be traced to this experience of redemption. "If any man be in Christ he is a new creature; old things are passed away, behold all things are become new," "Ye are all one in Christ Jesus." These are typical phrases of the New Testament, describing the intense form which the experience took in the earliest days. From the first it has had three aspects. (a) It is embodied in a redeemed community, whose members are bound together in a more intimate manner than is to be found in any other form of human society. (b) Within the community redemption moves primarily along personal lines, rebuilding individual character and deepening the natural gifts of personality; yet in such a way as to eliminate selfish individualism and build bridges of fellowship and mutual dependence. (c) The redemptive power which is at work is always traced to the action of God, and therefore involves a theological explanation of the whole experience. It was this third feature which, by the universal testimony of the earliest Christians, and by all Catholic theology ever since, is regarded as completely determinative for the Christian moral and social order. For the experience of redemption means for the individual a definite personal relationship of the soul to Christ; and it belongs to the essence of the experience that this relationship is not self-made. It comes through participation in the common life of the redeemed community. It is constituted by an act of Divine grace in baptism. It is personally realized and appropriated by acts of faith in Christ as the divine Redeemer from sin and Lord of life. This faith is primarily a personal attitude of devotion. But it is devotion to a Person whose life is shared by the whole redeemed community, and has been imparted to the individual soul only through membership in that community. By his acts of faith, therefore, the individual shares in a corporate communal life of faith. The object of his devotion is a historical Figure to whom the community is linked, not only by interior mystical experience, but by an external succession of historical events. Thus in the Catholic form of experience there is involved something else besides the purely personal attitude of faith, which Protestants inculcate. Inseparable from this personal attitude of faith is an acceptance of the historical tradition of the community as to the form which the redemptive action of God took in history.[1] For that which binds the community together is their common faith in God and knowledge of Him. And for that knowledge, as we have already seen, they are dependent, not only upon a revelation, but upon the definite form in which that revelation was given through a series of redemptive acts centering

[1] The course of historical criticism has shown that the modern inquirer cannot hope to get behind the judgment of the original community in interpretation of the Life of Christ, Cp. Bethune Baker, *Faith of the Apostles' Creed*, chapter i.

round the historical figure of Jesus Christ. This analysis shows why dogma must always have a fundamental place in a social order which is at the same time fully Christian, or, in other words, in any adequate embodiment of the Kingdom of God on earth. In defining the idea of the Kingdom of God above, it was said that with a "common recognition of God as the ground of human life goes a mutual dependence of men upon one another."[1] In the redeemed community we have found that this mutual dependence of individuals upon one another through a common faith in God involves a common acknowledgment of dogmatic statements about events in history. To this we may now add that besides assertion of events, such dogma must include a metaphysical interpretation of events. For the value of the events *for knowledge* is that their acceptance involves a particular view of God and His relations with the world. The Christian social values, then, are bound up with an experience of redemption which involves dogmatic beliefs. Dogmatic statements, such as the creeds, express so far as human language can, a body of truth about God and His dealings with man which is the basis of the religious experience of the community, and therefore the basis also of that type of social life which flows from such experience. Those who seek to disengage the Christian social ideals and their inspiration from their dogmatic and historical foundations are unscientific, because they ignore the testimony of those religious experiences which are our only source of information on the subject. They are also unpractical, because the distinctively Christian view of God came to us through a series of unique events in history, and has been preserved in dogmatic form. To cut away these historical and dogmatic elements means inevitably

[1] See page 66.

to exchange the Christian view of God for a vague doctrine of immanent spirit which has no sort of answer to the social problems of our day. For if God has not shown us that He transcends the sequence of natural events, then we have no ground for any hopes or aspirations which transcend the natural tendencies of civilization as we see them at work to-day.

But those whose outlook is inspired by the Catholic Creed are able to hope confidently for a social regeneration which utterly transcends the resources of human nature, because they find at work in themselves creative influences which are precisely of this supernatural quality. They believe that they share in a fellowship in which the Holy Spirit dwells. They believe that He pervades the personal life of each member of the community. In their personal experience of the workings of His grace they find a close analogy to the miraculous events of the Gospel. For them grace is not simply a vague immanent influence assisting the nobler impulses of human nature. Such an idea as that must always be in conflict with their normal experience. For the deepest element in that experience is not simply achievement of successful advance in the development of character, but a repeated impact of divine power upon human weakness. As ideals are pitched high, so the sense of natural human insufficiency to attain them is intensified. Yet failure is met again and again by the miracle of divine forgiveness, which absolves them of the past and renews in them that reconciliation with God which is the basis of their life in the community. Thus chains of habit are broken and new beginnings are continually made. At every moral crisis there descends upon the vacillating human will in its hour of temptation a power more than human, which recreates energy and renews hope of possibilities beyond natural expectation.

Thus moral progress is experienced, not as an achievement in conformity with nature, but as a divine gift which comes from beyond nature, and which carries the will to its end in defiance of natural tendencies. And the action of grace is experienced as a series of supernatural events, each of which embodies the creative power of God; the whole series transcending the ordinary series of natural events, to which it stands in the strongest possible contrast.

This action of the Holy Spirit upon human personality opens the way to the transformation of all personal relationships, for its range covers the whole community, and its tendency is to bring all into conformity with the moral ideal embodied in the life of Christ. But here we must note that this does not mean simply a process of imitation. It is true that one of the bonds uniting Christians together is their recognition of a common standard of morality. The foundations of that standard were laid in the Old Testament, and it was set forth finally in personal form in the life, acts, and words of Jesus Christ. But neither obedience to a moral code nor imitation of the highest ideal of character are in themselves sufficient to break down the barriers of individualism, to eliminate the isolating effects of egoism, and to weld men together into a living, world-wide, moral fellowship. Even social psychology is abandoning this artificial and external idea of imitation.[1] Moreover, it would offer a very inadequate explanation of the interior action of grace which we have been considering. For the Holy Spirit who thus transforms personality is the Spirit of Christ. His mission in the Church is to reproduce in human personality, not simply the principles or virtues exhibited in the life of Christ, but that very life itself. If virtue were men's

[1] Follett, *op. cit.*

true good, then grace would only need to bring them into conformity with an ideal pattern of humanity. Such a process would only be one of sanctified self-culture. Its end would be nothing but the self-centred perfection which formed the ideal of pagan ethics. But it is the mission of the Spirit to destroy such egoism, which is the greatest obstacle to the reign of God over human society. Moreover, regarded simply as an ideal example, the life of Christ could never be the pattern of mere ethical self-realization. For the outstanding feature of His earthly life is the sacrifice of the Cross; and the Cross makes havoc of all merely moral solutions of the social problem. It repudiates the various naturalistic western doctrines ancient and modern, which all alike postulate self-centred personality as the unit of society. But it repudiates also the idea of self-renunciation as an end in itself, or for any lesser end than the highest. The Cross declares as its principle the sacrifice of self to the glory of God, the surrender of self for the achievement of the divine purpose. This is a unique sociological principle which can never proceed from a doctrine of the natural immanence of divine Spirit.[1] It means the surrender of self, not to the spirit immanent in human society, but to Him who is above both self and society, at whose bar both must stand for judgment. It means the surrender of self to One whose will is the basis of objective right for all men. Yet self is not surrendered to abstract right, for the movement is on the higher plane of personal relationships. And thus it is that human life is actually achieved and finds itself through the surrender which the Cross claims from it. For it is only by the

---

[1] The idea that it can be grafted on to such a doctrine is the mistake made by Royce in *The Problem of Christianity*. It is also perhaps the characteristic error of current theological modernism.

sacrifice of self in surrender to the divine will that the egoism of self can be destroyed in such a way that personality is liberated. Sacrifice for any lesser end would be dangerous. But in yielding himself to God a man yields himself to the divine purpose for human society, and becomes truly himself in the measure in which he is made one with that purpose. Thus the sacrifice of the Cross embodies the deepest law of personal life.

Now, according to the Catholic doctrine of redemption, the Son of God brought this life-principle of the Cross out of the inner life of God down to the level of man, and there wrought it out Himself in His own life as an achievement at once divine and human. As God He did what man by himself never could do; and yet He did it also as Man on behalf of mankind. It was fitting that He who was born of a Virgin by a new creative act of God should thus, by another divine creative act through His death, bestow upon mankind a new spiritual possession, something so great and ultimate that it has never been adequately defined in words; but which makes possible at once the reconciliation of man with God and of men with one another. We must pass over deeper questions involved in this mystery of atonement and confine ourselves here to one fact. In the redeemed community the Holy Spirit imparts to human personality the life of Christ; not merely its life-principle of sacrifice, nor its human perfections, but the actual divine life of Him in whose image man was made and for whose glory he exists. Nothing less than this can be claimed as the inner meaning of the experience of redemption. Yet that which is imparted is the life of Christ crucified; and it is the Spirit's mission to reproduce the life of the Crucified in all men. Thus the aim of the Gospel is, in the first instance, neither to make men moral nor even

social, but to reintegrate the broken fragments of humanity by infusing into them the life of God. The infused life
is a crucified life which reproduces the mark of the Cross
upon human personality, making it flexible and capable
of fellowship through self-surrender. Yet the surrender
is first of all to God. It is not a social compromise; but
a consecration of personality to Him who is the ground
of both self and society. Thus all human relationships
are to be harmonized by a way which leads all men back
to God.

Thus far we have been considering the transformation
of personal relationships in society through an interior
redemption of personality. But the body and its outward connections have also a fundamental place in the
scheme of redemption. All social relationships are
through the medium of our bodily life. A full redemption of man, therefore, will take into its scope the whole
social structure and all the outward order of human
life as it is lived in the body. The dogma that "the Word
was made flesh" declares the goodness and value of
everything that belongs to the common life of man and
its outward expression. It reasserts the truth of Creation that "God saw everything that He had made, and
behold it was very good." The same truth is emphasized
in another way by the miracle of the Resurrection. The
body of the Lord was raised from the tomb as a natural
corollary of all that had gone before. When the Son of
God took a human body to Himself, He proclaimed the
sacredness of everything belonging to man's bodily life.
When, therefore, He had completed His redeeming act
of sacrifice on the Cross, His spiritual victory was most
appropriately declared not merely in survival of the soul,
but in a resurrection of the body. In this way it was
made plain that the whole of human life, body as well as

spirit, had been redeemed. Again, it was upon this fact of the resurrection that men's faith chiefly rested in the days when the new social order first appeared. On the strength of this fact they looked for a new era upon earth.[1] To those who believe in the resurrection it is natural to hope for a redemption of society. For it follows from this article of the Creed that material things have a permanent spiritual value and significance, and that there can be no true redemption of man's life unless his material existence be included. The same truth is enforced by the institution of the sacraments, which Catholics value highly because they bring the bodily life into the heart of religion, and make the most solemn religious acts to have a deeply social character. According to Catholic doctrine the sacraments are means whereby we receive divine grace through material things. Though people do not always understand the social significance of the Creed they profess as could be wished, the sacraments are generally understood among Catholics to mean that religion is a social force which has affinity with all true interests of human life and that it is capable of lifting these things to a higher level. The same cannot be said of those changes in religion which Protestantism introduced, and upon which it has nourished our present civilization. For it reduced religion to a private pietism which concerned the soul of man and not his body, the individual and not society as a whole; which set out to touch only a little circle of personal duties, not to effect the redemption and consecration of all that adorns human fellowship. It reduced theology to a rationalism which was unfettered by respect for common tradition. Thus it dissolved the authority of dogma, and left men free to build up all the relationships of life

[1] Acts iii. 13-21.

on a basis of opportunism and self-interest. Deeply rooted in this type of religion is the Manichean tendency, which divorces the soul from the body, because the material world is thought to be unworthy of being yoked to the life of the spirit. This tendency lies behind almost everything that is degrading in our modern civilization. It has developed, as we have already seen, a culture which is introspective and subjective in form; and it has handed over the external world to a mechanism separated from spiritual values, which mocks and denies all efforts of the human spirit to recover control over it.

In contrast to this, Catholicism with its doctrine of the resurrection of the body asserts that the subject to be redeemed is not simply the soul, but the whole world of human personality with its unity of body and spirit. A social order based on Catholic dogma would therefore reverse the whole of that tendency which in our present order drives a wedge of separation between spiritual realities and the material structure of society. That separation vitiates everything at present. It narrows the scope of religion and hinders it from its natural function of maintaining justice, liberty, and fellowship, and inspiring simplicity, craftsmanship, and art in every activity of life. It makes culture aristocratic and science materialistic. In religion those who have lost the sacramental tradition often find it hard to-day to see any value in the resurrection of the body. This is natural enough; for it is only Catholicism which, by making sacraments the centre of religious experience, provides its adherents with a constant present experience of the dignity of material things and their capacity for becoming the medium of spiritual values. Above all in the central rite of the Eucharist, where the highest religious act takes place, there is set forth a living symbol of what a restored Christendom would be. In that rite the redemptive value of God's sacrificial love is declared to be the basis of a new human fellowship. It is a world-wide fellowship of all men, in which all have the same privileges without distinction of nationality, sex, or class, because all are sons and daughters of God, and as such are admitted to His banquet in perfect equality. They hold communion with God and with one another through material gifts of Bread and Wine; a sign that there can be no true life of the spirit which is not democratic and social, capable of expressing itself through the common acts and habits of daily life. As this rite centres round the simplest and most universal acts of man— eating and drinking, so a restored Christendom will take for its norm not the power and interests of the few, but the elemental needs of the common people. This sacrament of simple acts is surrounded by Catholics with all the external beauty and dignity which human art can devise. So, too, in a restored Christendom all the common acts of daily life and labour will be redeemed from their present dependence upon a degrading economic system, which stifles the workers' natural pride in good work by depriving them of any human interest in their tasks. Worship and work will be redeemed from their present separation; for work will be done in the spirit of a great common act of worship. Each individual will contribute to the whole the best that is in him according to his capacity and in harmony with the common need. Thus a whole world of human skill and creative power will be redeemed from slavery to selfish material interests, and will furnish a sacrifice acceptable to God and beautiful in the eyes of men.

THE RETURN OF "THE KINGDOM OF GOD"

BY

Rev. P. E. T. WIDDRINGTON

Rector of Great Easton, Dunmow

SYNOPSIS

The influence of the Church negligible, not because of its divisions, but because it is not agreed as to the essential nature of its Gospel. If it is to regain its moral authority, its first duty is to make the fundamental character of its message clear. Is the Christian Gospel nextworldly or otherworldly? Is it world-denying or world-affirming? The apologia of Troeltsch an acknowledgment of

OUR STANDPOINT.

The breakdown of Western civilization due to the renunciation of God by the nations. The decadence of personal morality the inevitable consequence of the abandonment of religious sanctions as the basis of national life. Christian living postulates the background of a common life in which Christian values are embodied: the primitive Church and its organization; the Mediæval Church and its doctrine of the two polarities of God's activity. Revealed religion gives scanty countenance to the notion that spiritual values are independent of social justice. The Manicheism of the religious world not less than the Materialism of the non-religious world responsible for the present condition of things.

The purpose of this essay to demonstrate the Kingdom of God as the essential character of the Gospel, and that upon the effective republication of the Gospel depends the fate of civilization.

THE KINGDOM OF GOD.

A phrase with a history: embodies the purpose of God in relation to the world. St. Augustine's argument in *The City of God*. The Theocratic idea. The function of The Law. Montefiore quoted. The struggles of the two centuries before Christ and the development of the sense of Divine Purpose in history. The conflict one between Religion and Materialism. The Apocalyptists.

The phrase "The Kingdom of God" cannot be understood apart from its context. Attempts made in Christian circles to evacuate the phrase of its content, and make it a synonym for personal salvation and immortality. Dr. Glover's *Christ of Experience*.

Tendency of the religious world to import into the Gospels its own mentality—it confuses Jamnia with Galilee. The meaning of "basileia" to the average Jew of our Lord's day: a dominion inseparable from a domain. To the Jew, what was at stake was not the Sovereignty of God, but the actualization of that sovereignty in the world. The preaching of John the Baptist: practical not speculative. Josephus on the cause of John's imprisonment.

The Teaching of Our Lord.

He did not define "the Kingdom": assumed that men knew what it meant. Spoke as one who saw the meaning of Israel's ideals and whose interpretations were based on "the mind of the Divine Author of the Law." Emphasized the requirements of the Kingdom on the individual: a new righteousness and a new citizenship. Nevertheless, His purpose not the salvation of the individual as such, but his redemption into the Kingdom of God. Luke xviii. 20, 21 discussed.

The Kingdom a God-given Kingdom: the Kingdom of the Father. Cannot be established by force. "Force no attribute of God." Our Lord's dissociation of Himself from the turbulent and ugly nationalism of the time. Although the gift of God, admits the co-operation of human wills.

The Kingdom the Vision of Reality. Mr. Clutton Brock's book. This aspect of the teaching belongs to the early period of the ministry. Conversion, the result of the vision of the Kingdom.

The clarifications of the Kingdom idea made by our Lord: its universality and its recognition of sex equality.

The second stage of the teaching: after Cæsarea Philippi. In the first stage the Kingdom outlined: the method of its achievement occupies the second. In what sense was the Messianic consciousness of our Lord a development? Mark ii. 18-20, Luke iv. 16-22 from the outset associates the Kingdom with His person and work. His alleged hesitancy in avowing His Messiahship. His reticence and reserve. His transformation of the received ideas of the Messiah more drastic than His treatment of the Kingdom. For the Messiah of tradition He substituted Himself: the Suffering Servant of Deutero-Isaiah, and prepared for the Baptism of the Passion—the seal of His Messiahship. The Kingdom came out of the Passion, the Cross, the Resurrection, and the Ascension. It has no dynamic significance apart from them. It is the Messiahship of Jesus which gives to His teaching of the Kingdom its essentially "new" character.

THE KINGDOM AND THE CHURCH.

The Church a corollary of the Messiahship of Jesus. The Messianic Kingdom implies the continuance of a covenanted society. F. D. Maurice on the Church as the child of the Jewish polity. Dr. Hort's view of the relation of the Church to the Kingdom. The view of the first Christians. Apart from our Lord's claim to be Messiah, no doctrine of the Church in the Gospels.

The effects of the transference of the Gospel to Gentile soil. Gradual disuse of the phrase "Kingdom of God." St. Paul. The phrase infrequent in apostolic literature. This no proof that the hope of the Kingdom abandoned. Dr. Burkitt's contrast between Reformed Rabbinism and early Christianity. Chilianism: its influence and ultimate condemnation. St. Augustine registered the close of the process by which "not of this world" became "not for this world."

CONCLUSIONS.

The paramount task of the Church to remaster its message. Not "the Gospel" but "the Gospel of the Kingdom." . . . . The Kingdom of God regulative of our theology, the cardinal doctrine of our preaching and the touchstone by which all the activities of the Church are tested. This will involve a second Reformation.

Obstacles in the path of making the Kingdom the regulative idea of theology. The work of the Ritschlian School and the prejudice aroused. Dr. Orr's view. Dr. Candlish.

The defence of the Catholic Faith calls for a new apologetic. The two foes to-day, Manicheism in the Church and Materialism in society must be met.

The Church exists to promote the Kingdom, not to replace it. Neglect of this truth marred the great achievement of Mediæval Christendom. The Church became a usurpation and then a tyranny. The Church and its conception of sanctity. Detachment no excuse for shirking life's responsibilities. The revival of "vocation" as expressing the Christian demand on the ordering of society. The price of industrialism is the souls of men.

The Church must ever witness to the God-givenness of the Kingdom. Ozanam and the two theories of Progress.

CHAPTER IV

THE RETURN OF "THE KINGDOM OF GOD"
AT this time of economic and political crisis, the influence of organized Christianity on the affairs of the world is almost negligible. The cause is to be sought, not in the divisions of the Church—they furnish a contributory cause—but in the patent fact that the Church is not agreed as to the fundamental character of the Gospel. Before it can hope to regain its moral authority over the nations, it must first arrive at a common understanding concerning the essential nature of its message. Is the Christian religion next worldly or other-worldly? Is it a world-denying or a world-affirming faith? The widest divergence of opinion exists on these questions, and bewildered by the uncertain voice with which the Church speaks, men are ceasing to look to it for any guidance in practical affairs. Of what avail is it for the world to turn to the Church when they are told, by one of the foremost living Christian apologists,[1] that "Christianity has retired to the depths of the inner life, and at the same time risen to a height which transcends State and War and Culture—the union of souls in a sphere above the earth, the sphere of the Highest and the Ultimate? From thence Christianity still overcomes the world."

[1] Troeltsch, quoted by Von Hugel, *The German Soul*, p. 106.

To the writers of these essays the stupendous dis-
array of European civilization is due to the renunciation
of God by the nations, and their repudiation of the Catholic tradition of the vassalage of every nation to the
Kingdom of God.[1] To us, the decadence of personal
morality, believed by the devout within the Churches to
be due to the weakening of Faith in dogmatic religion,
is the inevitable aftermath of the abandonment at the
Reformation of religious sanctions as the basis of social
and international life. That Christian morality survived
so many centuries is a testimony to the social ethics of
Christendom.

Christian living postulates the background of a common
life in which Christian values are embodied. In Holy
Scripture the revelation of God is conditioned by the
existence of just relations among men. To this the New
Testament is no less a witness than the Old. Early
Christianity exhibited the phenomenon of an organized
community with a life of its own. The Mediæval Church,
by its doctrine of the two polarities of God's activity—
the State and the Church—secured the recognition of the
essentially religious character of the economic and other
relations of society. Revealed religion does not ask men
to make bricks without straw. One of the points by
which it is differentiated from the religions which men
have made for themselves is that it inheres in the common life, and gives scanty countenance to the notion
that spiritual and moral values are independent of social
justice. In modern times the religious world has suffered
from over-refinement: a result to some extent, in this
country, of its bourgeois environment. In the Ages of
Faith this over-refinement would have been called
"Manicheism." By whatever name it is called, its

[1] Wisdom, vi. 1-9.

results have been disastrous. They can be repaired only by a return to the central doctrine of Our Lord's teaching—the Kingdom of God. The purpose of this chapter is to demonstrate the Kingdom of God as the essential character of the Gospel; as a social conception at every stage of its development; and that the revival of the influence of the Church on national and international affairs will follow when once the Kingdom of God becomes the regulative idea of our theology and propaganda: to demonstrate, in a word, that upon the effective republication of the Gospel depends the fate of civilization.

"The Kingdom of God" is a phrase with a history. Saint Augustine argues in *"The City of God"*[1] that the Kingdom of God, of which Christianity is the completion, has always existed ever since there were men, and that it has a connected, though sometimes hidden existence, during the whole course of history. It is the motif which runs through the Holy Scriptures and makes of the Bible one book. The religion of Israel derived its unique force amongst the religions of the ancient world by reason of its faith in the sovereignty, the Kingship of God, and His purpose for human life. It is the glory of the Hebrew prophets and apocalyptists that they consciously apprehended and developed the idea around which the hopes of all mankind centre. What distinguished the Jewish people from the other peoples of antiquity was not "monotheism," but their unswerving conviction that this world was meant to be the scene of a Divine Order with ramifications in every department of life. They were the chosen instrument through which this Divine Order was to be achieved. The sin and the misery of the world was that it was living apart from the

[1] *De Civitate Dei*, xviii, 47.

Law of God. Their devotion to the Law rested on the
belief that the Law was given by God as the means of
enabling men to live in just relations. "The Law was
not a mere external law, fulfilled from fear of punish-
ment and for hope of reward. It was the law of the
All-Wise and all-righteous God, given to Israel as a
sign of supremest grace. It was a token of divine affection and its fulfilment was the highest human joy."[1] The
struggles of the two centuries before Christ intensified
these convictions. The conflict of Judaism with Græco-
Roman civilization was not merely the conflict of one
civilization with another. It was the conflict between
religion and materialistic civilization, fought on national-
istic lines. To the Jew with his unbroken tradition of
the Living God—the "I will become what I will
become"[2]—it was justice, God's justice, for which he
fought, and for the Moral Law revealed by God as
opposed to the *mores* of the Gentiles. In those two centuries the idea of the Kingdom exercised an increasing
influence on Jewish thought. It was the heroic epoch
of their national life. The Jews played a more prominent
part on the world's stage than they had ever occupied.
It was the turn which Jewish history took more than any
conscious process of thought which led to the explication
of the idea of the Kingdom, or, as it was commonly
called in the apocalyptic writings, "the coming age."
The world of the apocalyptists was a larger world than

[1] Montefiore, *Synoptic Gospels*, ii. 513.
[2] "I will become what I will become," Dr. Burney in *Contentio
Veritatis*, p. 181. The name Jehovah seems to mean "He who will
become," and that passage (Exodus iii. 13-15) in which the name
is elucidated by the statement, "I am what I am," or rather, "I
will become what I will become," implies that no words can adequately sum up all that the God of Israel *will become* to His chosen
people, etc. The reference is to Driver in *Studia Biblica* i. pp. 12 ff.

that of the prophets. In the Book of Daniel, as Mr. Edwyn Bevan has pointed out, "the great Gentile Kingdoms, like the Greek supremacy of the Seleucids and the Ptolomies, which seemed so overwhelming and terrible, are shown as phases in a world process whose end is the Kingdom of God."[1] The coming of the Kingdom of God is perceived to mean more than the triumph of Israel: it is triumph of Religion over Materialism, the visible justification of the ways of God to man. "The true and universal religion must be born of a nation, but it must rise above it."[2]

It is not germane to this essay to enter into a discussion of the phases through which the Apocalyptic Hope passed. The point I desire to emphasize is that "The Kingdom of God" in the Gospels is a phrase with a his-

---

[1] *Jerusalm under the High Priests*, p. 86. Cf. *The Beginnings of Christianity*, Foakes Jackson and Kirsopp Lake, p. 278. "The fact that the exact phrase, the Kingdom of God, is not found earlier than the Gospels, though the idea represented by it in the Rabbinic literature is drawn from the Prophets, renders it impossible to say with certainty what the phrase must have meant in the Gospels, and to use this meaning for their interpretation. The only reasonable method is to interpret each passage in which it is found in accordance with its context."

[2] Dr. Glover in his recent book, *The Christ of Experience*, is an example of this tendency in modern theology.

"Messiah was done into Greek, and became more a personal name than a description. . . . So while the title 'Christ' survived, the 'Kingdom of God' fell into the background, and in spite of efforts being made to bring it forward again, it is possible to maintain that 'salvation' was an expression that could carry a larger burden of Jesus' meaning. . . . What interested the Greek was not the restoration of a kingdom to a generalized Israel, or anything else, in the plural or abstract, but the development of his own soul, mind, and nature, and its securing amid all the changes of worlds and æons" (pp. 36, 7 and 8).

tory, and cannot be understood apart from that history.
For so much that has been written and is currently
believed in Christian circles either ignores the history of
the phrase or assumes that our Lord used it in a way and
placed upon it a connotation which divorced it from its
previous associations.   To all intents He might have
coined the phrase, or adapted any other which would
have expressed His ruling ideas of the sway of God in
the life of the individual, salvation, and immortality.   To
interpret the Kingdom of God apart from its context is
to cut off the teaching of Jesus from the great religious
tradition out of which it arose and of which it is the fulfilment.   Jettison the belief that "God at sundry times
and in diverse manners spake in time past unto the
prophets," and you undermine the faith of the Catholic
Church that "in these last days He hath spoken unto us

It is because the revival of the Kingdom as the regulative
principle of our theology and the motive of our propaganda will
purge the Church of associations with the modern equivalents of
Mystery Cults, Neo-Platonism, etc., and maintain the Catholic belief
in the Old Testament as containing a revelation independent of the
revelation of Jesus Christ, that we stress the necessity of insisting
on the historical antecedents of our Lord's teaching.

Cf. also Stalker's *Christology:* ". . . Although Jesus published His
Gospel under the form of a doctrine of the Kingdom of God, it may
be doubted whether He did this strictly on His own motion or rather
under stress of circumstances, adapting His teaching to the modes
of thought current in His time" (p. 25).

Notice the curious remarks on p. 166: "To many Christians,
living under republican forms of government, the very name is
foreign and out of date. Whatever be the case in Germany, to our
ears the phrase as a name for Christianity has a sound of preciosity
and make-believe; and there are far better names for the same
thing. . . . Jesus, before the close of His life, outgrew it; and His
teaching seems always trying to escape from its fetters. . . .The
phrase belongs, in short, to the 'body of humiliation'" (p. 165).

by His Son." Historical Christianity rests on the affirmation, "Salvation is of the Jews."

The tendency of the religious world is to import into the Gospels its own mentality. Its long sojourn at Jamnia[1] puts it at a grave disadvantage in any attempt to explore a situation in which religion was very intimately bound up with material things. The truth of this observation is demonstrated by a study of the bulk of the interpretations which have been made of the phrase "the Kingdom of God." That the word translated *basileia* means literally "Reign," and not the sphere in which the reign is exercised, is true. But to assume that in our Lord's day it meant "reign," rather than a definite sphere and polity in which the reign should be actualized, to any but a handful of pedants, is grotesquely untrue. To the average Jew the term connoted a dominion inseparable from a domain.[2] The proclamation of the Sovereignty of God, conceived as apart from the ordering of this world in righteousness, could not have been made the occasion of a preaching which secured a hearing from

---

[1] Jamnia was the village to which Johanan ben Zakkai retired during the siege of Jerusalem and where he settled to the task of reforming the Rabbinic religion by purging it of apocalyptic beliefs. The apocalyptic beliefs passed into the keeping of the Christian Church. Dr. Burkitt has drawn a striking contrast between Reformed Rabbinism and Early Christianity (*Jewish and Christian Apocalypses*, pp. 12-13). Modern Christians would be much more at home in the vineyard at Jamnia than in the fiercely expectant atmosphere of the early Christian Churches.

[2] Stanton, *The Jewish and the Christian Messiah*, p. 217. "Connection with the Old Testament preparation and Jewish hopes furnishes a complete answer to those who would translate 'Reign' instead of 'Kingdom of God.' Kingdom includes both ideas, that of His royal authority and of the realm over which He rules; and both should be included. Cf. also Burkitt in *Interpreter*, vol. vii. No. 4, p. 14.

Jews of the first century. The Jew had always believed in the sovereignty of God. What was at stake was the realization of that sovereignty in the world. "The Kingdom of God," to the masses of our Lord's contemporaries, meant the outward manifestation of God's sovereignty, by His overthrow of the evil powers which held the world in thrall and the establishment of a kingdom in which the ancient hopes of God's people should be fulfilled. Such was the substance of the Messianic idea. It had been vulgarized by politicians, physical force revolutionaries, and by apocalyptists. The bitter struggles for national freedom and the bloody reprisals they had brought had made the Jew vindictive and revengeful. He thought of God as an ally in his schemes of national aggrandisement. He forgot the nobler teaching of the prophets. To a not inconsiderable section of the Palestinian populace, insurrection had become a business, with brigandage as a side line.[1]

There were circles in which "the Hope and promises made to the fathers" had lost none of its purity—devout coteries at Jerusalem and elsewhere. Political unrest and the opinion that the Messianic Kingdom could not be long delayed were widespread. Everywhere there was a tense atmosphere of expectation. This is evident from the immediate response evoked by the preaching of the Baptist. The burden of his preaching was the imminence of the Kingdom, and an insistence on the moral repentance of the individual. Only the righteous Israelite could hope to enter into the blessings of the new order. The interest of the Baptist was practical. His mind was not speculative. He said nothing, as far as we know, to correct or amplify the current notions of the Kingdom. His concern was with the portentous fact that the King-

[1] Josephus, *Antq.*, xvii. 10, 8.

dom was near, and that men must make themselves ready for it. That the political revolutionaries made capital out of John's preaching to fan the flames of rebellion is probable, and borne out by the statement of Josephus that Herod threw John into prison "lest his influence might lead to some revolt."[1]

It is important for the argument of this essay to notice that the Baptist and our Lord are in agreement on a vital point concerning the Kingdom. They use the phrase as one which requires no definition. Both assume that men know what it is. In our Lord's teaching "the frequent formula 'the Kingdom of God is like' refers not to the nature of the Kingdom, but to the conditions on which it must be entered, the character of its members, the manner of its progress, the signs of its coming, etc." There is nothing in the Gospels to show that our Lord meant by "the Kingdom" something substantially different from what it meant to the men of his generation. If He did, then it was a mistake to have used the term. There were others He might have employed: "the Good Time," "the Days of the Messiah," or "the Age to Come." His deliberate adoption of the phrase brought him at once into touch with the common people stirred to enthusiasm by the Baptist's preaching. Our Lord was never at home with the professionally religious and the "cultured." This may have been a reason why He chose the phrase in which the common man summed up his faith in God and the world. But the real reason of His choice was that it linked on His teaching to that of the prophets and carried with it a scriptural consecration.[2]

From the outset of His ministry, our Lord stands out

[1] Josephus, *Antq.*, xviii. 5, 2.
[2] E. F. Scott, *The Kingdom and the Messiah*, chapter iv.

as an independent teacher. He speaks as an authoritative
interpreter; one who sees the meaning of Israel's ideals
and elucidates and clarifies them. His claim is to fulfil
the Law and the Prophets. There is no hesitancy in His
claim. His rulings are "based on the mind of the divine
author of the Law."[1] He places a new emphasis on the
aboriginal and illimitable worth of the individual. He
stresses and elaborates the requirements the Kingdom
makes on those who would be its citizens. For the legal
righteousness of His day He substitutes the new righteousness of the Kingdom with its motive "that ye may be
the sons of your Father in heaven." Although insistent
on the inalienable value of the single soul, He, nevertheless, teaches that the purpose of the Father is not primarily the salvation of individuals as such, but their union
in the redeemed society of the Kingdom of God. The
Kingdom never ceases to be a collective hope: a conception involving the life of man in all its relations "as
broad as human life, as deep as human need." The
attempt that has been made, on the strength of one saying, to make the Kingdom merely a synonym for an inward state of blessedness must now be regarded as a
failure.[2] Not even the authority of Matthew Arnold can
save it.

The Kingdom is the Kingdom of the Father. It rests
on the character and nature of God. From the beginning
it has been the purpose of God in history to permeate the
life of man with the principles which belong to His character: to educate man into correspondence with "the
world of invisible laws by which He is ruling and blessing

[1] Kirsopp Lake, *op. cit.* p. 294.
[2] Luke xviii. 20 Cf. Shailer Mathews, *The Social Teaching of
Jesus,* p. 46 (*note*); E. F. Scott, *op. cit.* p. 108 ff; Plummer's
St. Luke, p. 406.

His creatures."[1] Men have not of themselves the power
to establish the Kingdom. It cannot, for instance, be
established by force. "Force," as an early Christian
apologist well said, "is no attribute of God." The Kingdom requires the consent of human wills. But while the
Kingdom is the gift of God and His work, its coming
can be accelerated by the faith and co-operation of men.

How decisively our Lord dissociated Himself from the
turbulent nationalism of his day is brought out in the
indignant question he puts to those who carried out his
arrest. "Are ye come out, as against a robber (ὡς ἐπὶ
λῃστήν) with swords and staves to take me?" λῃστής is not
the word for an ordinary robber, but for a member
of a guerilla band. The "Penitent Thief" who was
crucified with our Lord was a member of such a band.
His repentance was repentance in the strict sense of
metanoia. He had been a believer in the cruder forms
of nationalism. The reproaches which he and his com-
rade hurled at Jesus were for not having helped them in
their revolt against the foreign oppressor. As he hung on
his cross, he came to understand the true nature of the
Kingdom, and hails Jesus as its Messiah.[2]

There is an aspect of our Lord's teaching to which
sufficient attention has not been paid: the Kingdom as
the Vision of Reality. It may belong to the first stage
of the teaching—the stage which Baron Von Hugel[3]

[1] Hort, *Life and Letters,* vol. ii. p. 273.

[2] Cf. the illuminating remarks in *The Beginnings of Christianity.*
Part I, p. 289 ff., on our Lord's definite opposition to the policy of
armed rebellion against the foreign oppressor, and the significance
of the "non-resistant" teaching in the Sermon on the Mount. Also
Savage's *Gospel of the Kingdom,* p. 6. Plummer's *St. Luke* (International Critical Commentary), on Luke xxiii. 39-43, and West-
cott's *Some Lessons of the R.V.,* p. 76.

[3] Von Hugel, "Essay on Progress in Religion" in *Progress and
History,* edited by F. S. Marvin, p. 114.

describes as "predominantly expansive, hopeful, peace-fully growing," to the stage of "the plant parables, full of exquisite sympathy with the unfolding of natural beauty," but it is not to be neglected. Whatever may be the defects of Mr. Clutton Brock's book, *What is the Kingdom of Heaven?* it has recalled to us this fact, that our Lord insisted that the Kingdom was something which men might see, if they would, here and now. The pure in heart shall see God, and God is to Christ "the Kingdom of Heaven in its utmost intensity, the reality at the heart of that reality." Conversion as He taught it is the result of the vision of the Kingdom: it is a change of mind under a new impression of the facts of life, a new orientation. Our Lord always speaks as one who sees the Kingdom. He is amazed at the blindness of those about Him.

> 'Tis ye, 'tis your estranged faces
> That miss the many splendoured thing.

It is not necessary to dwell on His attitude towards the class distinctions of his time, and His identification of Himself with those that labour and are heavy laden.[1] He illustrated in His own conduct the new law of brother-liness: "love on the footing of equality." Nor, again, need we insist on the sternness of his views on riches and of the effects of covetousness on the soul. But there are two clarifications of the idea of the Kingdom which must be noticed: its universality and its recognition of sex equality. Jesus transcended the narrow nationalism of contemporary Judaism. The new wine of the King-dom fermenting in the mind of Jesus broke the old bottles

[1] Our Lord and His disciples must have been regarded by the Scribes and Pharisees among the *ame ha-ares.* Cf. *Beginnings of Christianity*, App. E. on "The Am Ha-ares."

of Jewish particularism. John had insisted that not descent from Abraham, but moral righteousness was the passport into the new order. Our Lord carried the teaching of John to its logical conclusion. If moral righteousness were the passport, then men everywhere had "kingdom capacity." The field of the kingdom was the world. The second clarification was not less astounding: the admission of women to equality of citizenship. Whatever may have been the case amongst the Jews of the Dispersion, Palestinian Judaism had steadily depressed the status of women. Our Lord brushed on one side the traditions of men. He recognized no superiority of the male personality over that of the female. He appealed to both men and women with the same arguments. The most profound of all his sayings was addressed to a woman. His attitude surprised His disciples as greatly as it offended His opponents. "They marvelled that He talked with a woman."[1] What is of paramount importance to the understanding of our Lord's teaching of the Kingdom is His own relation to it. Never was this more the case than at the present moment.

We have seen that our Lord grouped his teaching around the idea on which all the hopes of His people had come to centre. He follows up the preaching of the Baptist. He develops His work. He comes forward as a reinterpreter of the Law, and elucidates its meaning by a criticism, humane, penetrating, inspired. He reawakens the sense of vision in a people in whom, owing to the weight of an authoritarian religion, vision was almost dead. He revitalizes the doctrine of the Fatherhood of God in such a way as to make men understand that the Kingdom was dependent on the loving purpose of God, and that on that purpose rather than on the

[1] St. John iv. 27.

activities of men rested the certainty of its achievement.
Lastly, we have glanced at two instances illustrating the
clarifications our Lord effected in the current conceptions of the Kingdom.   But so far we have dealt with
only one stage of the teaching.

The incident at Cæsarea Philippi is the dividing line
between the two stages of our Lord's ministry.   In the
first stage the Kingdom has been outlined.   The method
of its achievement is now the dominant theme.   From now
onwards the Messianic character of the Kingdom is increasingly stressed.   The term "Son of Man" is used
in a definitely Messianic sense.   The Passion is predicted.
Our Lord sets Himself to two tasks: to brace Himself
for the Baptism which awaits Him at Jerusalem and to
prepare the minds of the disciples for the supreme revelation of the Love and Power of God.

The division of our Lord's ministry into two stages
does not imply that in the earlier stage He had no knowledge of His Messiahship.   It does imply that that knowledge underwent growth.   In this it differed from His
sense of Sonship which was a constant and unchanging
experience—"a unique consciousness of a unique relation."   At both stages of His ministry He associated the
Kingdom with His Person and work.   From the outset,
unless we are to displace Mark ii. 18-20, He had the fore-
boding of a tragic end to His career.   The story of the
Temptation, if we disallow the view that the accounts
in Matthew and Luke are coloured by subsequent events,
indicates that the problem of reconciling the accepted
ideas of Messiah with the intimations of His own consciousness, was with Him then.[1]   The precise moment

---

[1] Professor Burney, in a sermon entitled *The Old Testament Conception of Atonement Fulfilled by Christ* (1920), has drawn attention
to the Messianic significance of the incident in Luke iv, 16-22.

when He became fully aware of what His acceptance of
the Messianic rôle entailed, may be uncertain: the fact
that He accepted the rôle is clear. For the proof "is not
confined to a few isolated passages which might easily
be eliminated, but lies at the heart of the narrative, and
is meant to constitute its whole significance."[1] The
reasons for His hesitancy in openly avowing his claim I
do not propose to enter on. The reticence which He
observed may not be easy to explain, but we are not therefore compelled to accept explanations which make the
consciousness of His Messiahship a late development.
This is certain: "He felt that He stood in a unique relation to mankind, because He was chosen of God to be
the vehicle to them of the revelation of His Mind and
Will, to inaugurate a new era in the history of the world,
and, at whatever cost to Himself, to be the means by
which the Divine Order of human society, an order of
righteousness, mutual help, and brotherhood, should be
established."[2] It is not hard to see how His Messianic
claim had its roots in His Message of the Kingdom.

The change which our Lord wrought in the conception

"The passage in Isa. lxi. which begins with the words 'The Spirit
of the Lord is upon me, because He anointed me to preach good
tidings to the poor' . . . occurs in a group of chapters which are
not the work of Deutero-Isaiah but of a later post-exilic prophet,
who is, however, undoubtedly taking up and developing the earlier
prophet's conception of the ideal servant. . . I do not know how
the Lucan narrative is understood by those who hold that the
Synoptic Gospels witness to the fact that our Lord concealed His
Messianic claims in the earlier stages of His ministry, and in fact
until just before His Passion; but it certainly appears from it that
at a very early stage He was ready, before a suitable audience, to
proclaim Himself Messiah in the sense in which He understood and
assumed Messiahship."

[1] E. F. Scott, *op. cit.* p. 169.
[2] Bethune Baker, *Faith of the Apostles' Creed*, p. 57.

of the Messiah is the most startling and revolutionary
thing in His teaching. It is the unfolding of the content
of His Messianic consciousness which gives to His teaching of the Kingdom its essentially "new" character. He
transfused the Messianic conception with His own spirit.
He brought it into line with His own idea of kingliness.
At length, after deep travail and perplexity of soul, He
revealed His secret to His disciples and spoke of the
Baptism with which He must be baptized before He could
enter upon His destined office. He takes to Himself the
words of the Suffering Servant and interprets them as
Messianic. "The Messiah a Servant. Not so had kingship been conceived. The Suffering Servant of the
Prophet had not yet been commonly identified—if even,
as yet, identified at all—with the Messiah."[1] He declares
that by His death He will effect the coming of the Kingdom and render possible the life He has revealed to them.
That life was more than a mere emancipation from material disabilities: it was redemption into the life of God.
In a single phrase He epitomized the whole idea of the
great chapter of Isaiah: of God's purpose fulfilled by
one who dies for the common deliverance,[2] i.e. "give His
life a ransom for many." At the Last Supper He antici-
pates the New Covenant to be established through His
death. His death, Resurrection, and Ascension were the
establishment of a New Covenant, the setting up of the
Kingdom, and His Own enthronement as Messiah. The
Kingdom comes out of the crucible of the Passion and the
Resurrection. It has no meaning, and could have had
no existence apart from them.

It is at this point we can most conveniently pass to the
consideration of the Church. The Church is a corollary

[1] C. G. Montefiore, *Liberal Judaism and Hellenism*, p. 104.
[2] Mark x. 43.

of belief in the Messiahship of Jesus. The Messianic Kingdom implies the continuance of a covenanted Society.

Our Lord's hope had been that the Jewish Church would rise to its mission. It was only after its apostasy was demonstrated that He began the training of the Twelve for their office in His Ecclesia which is less a new creation than the completing and fulfilling of the Ancient Church of God. You cannot cut off the entail which binds the Christian to the Jewish Church. "The Church," as Frederick Denison Maurice says, 'was to the early Christians, certainly to the writer of the Acts, the child which the Jewish polity had for so many ages been carrying in its womb." The Church is the new Israel, the herald and instrument of the Kingdom. "We may speak of the Ecclesia as the visible representative of the Kingdom of God, or as the primary instrument of its sway, or under any other analogous forms of language. But we are not justified in identifying the one with the other, so as to be able to apply directly to the Ecclesia whatever is said in the Gospels about the Kingdom of Heaven or of God."[1] The Church was to the first believers the "Way" in which the laws of the Kingdom were in operation: it was the "community of the Messiah and therefore the New Israel." What was involved in those premises was not clear to them, but it was from these premises that the Catholic Church was evolved. Apart from the acceptance of these premises, it will always be open to men to argue that Our Lord did not found a Church, and that ecclesiastical Christianity is foreign to His intention. You cannot, if you expunge the belief in our Lord's claim to be the Messiah, build up a doctrine of the Church from the Gospels. The facts of the training of the Twelve and the Incident at Cæsarea Philippi are insuf-

[1] Hort, *The Christian Ecclesia*, p. 19.

ficient in themselves. The interpretation of certain parables as parables of the Church rather than as what they profess to be, parables of the Kingdom, is arbitrary and unjustifiable. There is no ground in the first chapter of the Acts for believing that the teaching after the Resurrection was concerned with the details of Church polity. "We do not need any special passages to prove that Jesus intended to found a religious society. It was implicit in his claim to be Messiah."[1]

The Church, almost from the start, found itself plunged into conflict and battling for its very existence. Absorbed by that conflict, aliens from their own mother's sons, treated with suspicion wherever they went, it is easy to see how the Church, in the minds of its members, tended to take the place of the Kingdom as the sphere in which the blessings of the New Age were to be enjoyed. Again, as Ritschl observes,[2] "Cares about the formation of congregations came so much to the front, that the entire moral interest was concentrated on their internal consolidation." The opening up of the Gentile world brought with it the problem of translating the idea of the Kingdom into the language of peoples to whom the belief in the effective sovereignty of God was unfamiliar. That the Gospel of the Kingdom lost something in its transmission to Gentile soil was inevitable and is evident from the study of the Pauline Epistles. That it was preached is proven.

When we reach the writings of the Apostolic Fathers, the Kingdom has receded into the background. With the exception of a saying of our Lord concerning the coming of the Kingdom in the so-called Second Epistle of Cle-

[1] Hamilton, *People of God,* vol. ii. p. 19.
[2] Ritschl, *Justification and Reconciliation,* edited by Mackintosh, p. 284.

ment,[1] references are few and far between. But the absence of references to the Kingdom in post-apostolic literature, does not mean that Christians were not awaiting and working for the Coming Age. "In the cities of the Empire, in the churches whose membership was drawn from the slave class and the poorer freemen, the belief was steadfast. "The Kingdom of God is at hand." A new world, a wholly new state of things is on the point of arriving; watch and be ready, and above all, do not cumber yourselves with your old possessions, your old traditions, your old affections."[2] Chilianism was a mighty influence amongst the rank and file of the Church. It claimed not a few (for instance, Irenæus) of the ablest men among its adherents. For four centuries at least the hope of the Kingdom, the common substance of which is the conviction that an order of life is possible on the earth in which righteousness, love, and peace are sovereign, maintained itself.[3] Then with the condemnation of Millenialism, the faith in the Kingdom began to decay, and with St. Augustine is completed the formal identification of the Church with the Kingdom. The Vision Splendid melted away until the Kingdom became "not for this world." It had always been, and must always be, "not of this world."[4]

[1] "The Lord Himself, being asked when His kingdom would come, said, 'When the two shall be one, and the outside with the inside, and the male with the female, neither male nor female.'"

[2] Burkitt, *Jewish and Christian Apocalypses*, p. 13. "I am not asking you to forget the personal influence of Jesus upon those who accepted Him as their Master, for indeed without it you lose the cord that both binds the Christians together and supplies the current of their enthusiasm. But that enthusiasm of the early Christians was directed to the Good Time Coming."

[3] Bethune Baker, *op. cit.* p.51-53

[4] "This putting off to another life in another world of the hope

I started with the plea that the paramount duty of the Church is to agree on the essentials of its message. For generations past the Church has preached what is called "the Gospel." The call to-day is to return to what the New Testament calls "the Gospel of the Kingdom"— the Kingdom of God, the cardinal doctrine of our preaching, regulative of our theology, and the touchstone by which all the activities of the Church are tested. This will involve a Reformation in comparison with which the Reformation of the sixteenth century will seem a small thing.

The task of building up our theology around the idea of the Kingdom is one requiring courage and presenting serious difficulties. It has been rendered more difficult than it necessarily is owing to the prejudice aroused by Ritschl and his school.[1] We shall be told that such a system will lead to the loss of essential values: that we are minimizers and dangerous persons. Notwithstanding all the difficulties which are alleged, the task must be undertaken.[2] It is necessary for the defence of the Catholic Faith. For it will enable us to meet the arguments, so speciously advanced, which make of the Faith a syncretism of rather dubious Oriental beliefs. The Catholic Faith stands or falls by the truth of the revelation of God contained in the Old and New Testaments. If St. Augustine found the key to that revelation in the development of the idea of the Kingdom, surely we have grounds for believing that such a task has reason behind it?

of the Kingdom and the realization of its conditions is perhaps the greatest apostasy that the history of religions can disclose." *Op. cit.* p. 52; Hort, *Christian Ecclesia*, p. 19.

[1] The topic is discussed by Dr. Orr, *Christian View of God and the World*, Appendix, "The Idea of the Kingdom of God."

[2] Cf. Candlish, *The Kingdom of God*, pp. 2-3.

Further, each age demands of the Church a new apologetic framed to meet its conditions. The two foes the Church must defeat are Manicheism within its own borders, and Materialism in the world outside.

We cannot blind our eyes to the fact that there exists within the Church a large body of opinion which is sub-Christian, and whose real creed is a crude "salvationism." It offers no hope of a better world. It ignores the social nature of the Gospel. It regards the Kingdom as a purely spiritual idea. But, "to suppose that Christ meant by His Kingdom a purely ideal state, which would have no earthly expression as a society, is to say that the Apostles and subsequent generations of His followers misunderstood him."[1] Such a supposition cuts human experience in two. It disparages the present life and makes it a mere antecedent to the future, robbing it of intrinsic dignity and worth. It rests on a conception of "the individual" which is philosophically false: "The individual soul" of the pietist is as much an abstraction as the "economic man" of the Classical economists. To quote a non-Christian writer, Mr. G. D. H. Cole: "The odd fact that man is at once soul and body forces itself into every social relationship, and binds together spirit and matter in a fashion which the philosophers have found it infinitely troublesome to explain. It is the most vicious of abstractions to take an aspect of human life and say of it: 'This at least is purely material.' That is, in a very real sense, 'the sin against the Holy Ghost.'[2] The theology of the Kingdom would purge the Church of that plausible insincerity which masquerades as "spiritual religion." As Ruskin told the clergy, "It would be well if many of us, in reading that text, 'The Kingdom of God

[1] Freemantle, *The World the Subject of Redemption*, p. 111.
[2] Cole, *Labour in the Commonwealth*, pp. 31-32.

IS NOT meat and drink,' had even got as far as to understand that it is at least as much, and that until we have
fed the hungry, there was no power in us to inspire the
unhappy."[1]

The Church must have the courage of its Baptismal
Creed with its first dogmatic assertion concerning Jesus
that He is the Christ, the Messiah whose special function
is to inaugurate on earth the Kingdom of God. It must
recognize that it is a means and not an end in itself.[2] Its
end is the Kingdom of God. So long as men serve the
Church first and what it should promote second, they are
not loyal to the Kingdom of God. There is an excusable
tendency to exaggerate the great achievements of the
Middle Ages, and to see in mediæval civilization a
Christendom as near perfection as is possible in this imperfect world. But why did mediæval civilization
collapse? There are reasons and reasons. I hold the
true one to be because at the root of that civilization there
was a lie. Mediæval civilization identified the Church
with the Kingdom of God. The Church, instead of
promoting the Kingdom, replaced it. The usurpation of
the Church and its disparagement of the other modes
through which the Kingdom is built, brought with it the
inevitable consequence. Catholicism degenerated into
the slavish worship of its own organization, and that

---

[1] Ruskin, *Letters to the Clergy*, p. 22.

[2] "Modern pietists are accustomed to describe their favourite
undertakings, especially foreign missions, directly as the Kingdom
of God, but in doing so, while they touch the ethical meaning of the
idea, they narrow its reference improperly. This circle, too, has
brought the word into use to describe, e.g. the public affairs of the
Church. . . . This use of the name involves the interchange of
Church and the Kingdom which we find dominating Roman Catholicism," and the writer might have added, "and Anglo-Catholicism."
Ritschl, *op. cit.* p. 11.

organization became a tyranny from which men at length revolted. The danger is not altogether a thing of the past. It has assumed a different form. The fact that the Church is an institution with large vested interests subjects it to the temptation of all large vested interests— the temptation to make the protection of its own material well-being the dominating influence in its policy. Again, the Church has suffered its conception of sanctity to become stereotyped. The outlook of the devout tends to grow narrowed the more they advance in what is called the "spiritual" life. Detachment is not infrequently misunderstood, and used as an excuse for avoiding the obligations of the common life. The intellectual meanness and narrow-mindedness of many of our devout people, both priests and laymen, are notorious. "So few make holiness in any sense their chief end that it may seem rash to speak against this, yet it is painfully true that even Christian faith becomes insipid and ineffective unless it confronts the world and is proved in the actualities and conflicts of life." [1] With a new orientation of our theology would come the recognition that the Kingdom which is being built is built up through the exercise of diverse gifts of the One Spirit, and we shall no longer standardize spirituality.

One of the encouraging signs of the times is the revival of the idea of "vocation" in relation to the ordinary pursuits of life. If it is applied faithfully, it will, I am convinced, do more to awaken the social conscience of churchmen than all the appeals which have hitherto been made. It is better so. Social endeavour should not rest on the fear for public stability, but on a reverence for immortal souls. [2] The idea of "vocation" faithfully applied

[1] Dr. Denney.
[2] Bussell, *Christian Theology and Social Progress*, p. 94.

will reveal to the sincere but obscurantist Christian the appalling extent to which the present industrial system renders the idea inconceivable to multitudes of his fellow-men. How are men to develop the sense of vocation in the useless toil on which they are forced, through economic compulsion, to waste their energies? Boys

> Our life is turned
> Out of her course, wherever Man is made
> An offering or a sacrifice, a tool
> Or implement, a passive thing employed
> As a brute mean, without acknowledgment
> Or common right or interest in the end;
> Used or abused as selfishness may prompt.[1]

forced into blind alley occupations; men and women engaged in the production of goods which it is an insult to a free man to have to produce, lives without interest and with no self-determination—spent in an environment which degrades the soul and injures the body—how, and in what sense are these to be taught the glory of the common life and the surpassing dignity of service?

Nor is the evil confined to the working hours: it affects the leisure time. The higher instincts are numbered and the whole life is vulgarized. "The greatest crime of our industrial and commercial civilization is that it leaves us a taste only for that which can be bought with money, and makes us overlook the purest and sweetest joys which are all the while within our reach."[2]

The Church, once delivered from ecclesiastical-mindedness and aflame with the faith of the Kingdom, will be compelled to adopt towards our industrial system the same attitude which our missionaries take towards the

[1] Wordsworth, *The Excursion*, Book IX.
[2] Sabatier (Paul), *St. Francis*, p. 107.

social order of heathendom. It will then challenge the Industrial World as it challenged the forces of Roman Imperialism in the days of persecution.

We dare not deceive ourselves. That brighter and more perfect future, the consummation of the Kingdom of God, is only to be reached through much tribulation. God is the Maker of it. He has made it already in His Son. We are His fellow workers in bringing it to pass. The Church is the social leaven of the twice-born. "There are in reality only two doctrines of progress: the first, nourished in the schools of self-indulgence, seeks to rehabilitate the passions; and promising the nations an earthly paradise at the end of a flowery path, gives them only a premature hell at the end of a way of blood; the second, born and inspired by Christianity, points to progress in the victory of the spirit over the flesh, promises nothing but as the prize of warfare, and pronounces the creed which carries the warfare into the individual soul to be the only way of peace to the nations."[1]

[1] Ozanam.

THE MEDIÆVAL THEORY OF SOCIAL ORDER

BY

Rev. A. J. CARLYLE, D.Litt.

Author of *Mediaeval Political Theory in the West*, Vol. I.-IV., etc.

CHAPTER V

THE MEDIÆVAL THEORY OF SOCIAL ORDER

THERE may be considerable dispute as to the precise character of mediæval civilization. To the good people of the Renaissance it seemed to be a mere barbarism, and perhaps the sentimental conceptions about it, common during the Romantic period, were almost as far from the truth. For the Middle Ages, as we are beginning to see, present us with a spectacle of bewildering complexity; men were brutal, ferocious, immoral, and often ignorant; but at the same time they were fired by a passion for beauty, which transformed almost everything that they touched; they were indefatigable in their pursuit of truth, and they were often possessed by a sense of the spiritual. And, whatever were their shortcomings, they did at least believe firmly that the first and last principle of social life was justice.

It is upon this that I am glad to have the opportunity to say a little. I do not suppose that my own judgment upon the mediæval world or Church would correspond precisely with that of other writers in this volume, but I should agree with them in thinking that we have not yet recovered from the foolishness of the eighteenth century, and that we have a good deal to learn from a time when men did not confuse utility with principle, or imagine that the world advances by the reckless pursuit of self-interest. And perhaps to-day, when it seems clear that that illusory

theory of the absolute sovereignty of the State, which
was developed by the eccentric genius of Hobbes, and
more or less accepted by some jurists in England and
America, is breaking down, it may be useful to remind
ourselves of a time when this conception of sovereignty
was not merely unknown, but would have seemed to
serious men a form of lunacy.

For the first, and in some ways the most essential aspect
of the normal political thought of the Middle Age was
that it knew nothing of absolute authority except the
authority of justice, which was generally conceived of as
being embodied in the law. In the State, as we should
now call it, the king was not supreme, but the law, and in
the Church it was not the Pope, but again the law; and a
law, whether of Church or State, was null and void if it
was contrary to the law of nature, which Gratian
identified with the law of God.

It may seem paradoxical to those who are not familiar
with the literature and the political life of the Middle
Ages, but the real truth about them is that men knew
nothing of an arbitrary and capricious authority, while in
the deplorable confusions of the period of the Renaissance
many Romanists and High Anglicans, and some Protestants, persuaded themselves to accept an arbitrary mon-
archy, and in our own day there is some danger lest we
should imagine that we believe in an arbitrary absolutism
of democracy. The most serious danger of modern
society is not, as some very short-sighted critics imagine,
the tendency to anarchy, but the desire to find some
absolute and final authority. It is the doctrine of absolute authority which is the greatest danger of our time,
and it is not less dangerous when it masquerades under
the form of democracy.

The first · principle of mediæval society was the

supremacy of justice; and justice was conceived of as embodied in law. The king, Bracton says, has two superiors, God and the law. This is the real meaning of the continual insistence upon justice as the rationale of kingship, which we find throughout the political literature of the Middle Ages from the ninth century onwards. The Abbot Smaragd, for instance, says: "Keep justice, O King, and judgment, this is the royal way trodden by the kings of old time. . . If thou desirest that God should establish thy throne thou shalt not cease to do justice to the poor." And the treatise, *De duodecim abusivis saeculi,* probably of Irish origin, which is frequently quoted in the ninth century, warns the king that he must not be unjust, but must restrain the unjust; it is the proper purpose of his office to rule, but how can he rule and correct others unless he first corrects himself. Justice in the king means to oppress no man unjustly, to judge righteously between men; to defend the weak, to protect the Church, to put just rulers over the kingdom; to live in God and the Catholic faith, and to keep his children from evil.

What such writers say was only repeated again and more emphatically by Bracton in the thirteenth century. The king, he said, is elected for this very purpose that he should do justice to all men, and that through him God may administer his judgments. The king is God's vicar upon earth, and it is his duty to divide right from wrong, the equitable from the inequitable, that all his subjects may live honestly and that no man should injure another. The king, therefore, should obey the authority of law (or right), as being the vicar and servant of God, for that alone is the authority of God: the authority of wrong belongs to the devil and not to God, and the king is the servant of him whose work he does. Therefore when the king does justice he is the vicar of the eternal King, but he is the servant of the devil when he does wrong.

We can put this into modern, more abstract terms, if we say that the primary function of the State is a moral function; that its primary end is the establishment of some moral order. This does not mean that we ignore what may be called the economic functions of organized society, but it does mean that we look upon them as subordinate to its moral function and end. And I venture to say that it is really high time that men should face this more resolutely. It has been said by men of some economic authority that Western civilization is at the present time faced with a dilemma, it can be either rich or free, but it cannot be both. There are perhaps some people who would put the dilemma under other terms and say that we can be either rich or just, but not both. As an historical critic I profess I am profoundly sceptical of such dilemmas. I do not think that the experience of the world really affords any justification for the opinion that any society can in the long run be rich which is not attempting to be free and just. But, supposing the dilemma to have some truth, we shall do well to ask ourselves which it is that we choose. There is at least no doubt about the principle of the Middle Ages.

To return to our immediate subject. To the mediæval thinkers, the idea of justice was not a mere abstraction, for justice was embodied in the law. We may indeed think that their conception of the living movement of the world was limited and inadequate, but at least they did believe in some concrete system of order and right in life.

I have already mentioned Bracton's great principle that the king had two superiors, God and the law, and it is worth while to look at this a little more closely. For to him the conception of that justice which the king must obey was not something elusive and intangible. In the first place and before all justice meant that which is expressed in the law, and without this Bracton could not conceive of authority at all. In another famous and admirable phrase he says, there is no king when will (that is capricious and arbitrary will) rules, not law; there is no such thing as authority in society, if it is an arbitrary one. The king is under law precisely because he is God's vicar, for Jesus Christ whom he represents on earth willed to be under the law that He might redeem those who were under the law. The Blessed Virgin thus also submitted to the ordinances of the law. The king should follow these examples; there is no man greater than the king in administering justice, but he should be as the least in receiving the judgment of the law.

It is this clear hold upon the first principle of a reasonable order which explains how firmly these mediæval thinkers could deal with the question of what was to be done if the ruler refused to carry out the law. The Assizes of Jerusalem do not hesitate either to lay down the principle, or to suggest how the principle should be enforced. The king, they say, has sworn to maintain the good usages of the kingdom, to protect the poor as well as the rich in the enjoyment of their right; if he breaks his oath he denies God, and his vassals and the people should not permit this, for the lord is lord only of law (or right) and not of wrong. And, to their minds, the method of compulsion was simple; they should withdraw their allegiance, and should refuse to carry out any of their feudal obligations until he submits.

This is again the meaning of that conception of political society as an association of mutual obligation which is the proper characteristic of the principles of mediæval life; this is the meaning of the continual insistence upon the mutual oaths of king and people which constituted the essential aspect of the coronation ceremony, and out of which there grew the historical theory of the social contract; not of course the confused and unhistorical conception of the seventeenth and eighteenth centuries. For this is the plain truth, the mediæval theory of organized society was the theory of a contractual relation, a relation of mutual obligation and service. This is obviously true of all feudal relations, but it was equally true of the larger political relation, which was for a time practically overlaid by feudalism, but which was older than feudalism and survived it.

It is thus again that John of Salisbury finds it easy to distinguish between the king and the tyrant, for the king is one who governs according to the law, who maintains and enforces and obeys it, while the tyrant is one who rules by violence, who overrides the law, and thus reduces the people to slaves. The king bears the image of God, the tyrant that of the devil.

And now, lest we should misunderstand this conception of law, we must remind ourselves that to these people law was not an arbitrary or irrational thing, representing the caprice of the ruler, or even of the people. We may consider it under two terms, each important and significant.

In the first place we many say that the law did not normally present itself to the people of the Middle Ages as a thing that was made. Law was primarily custom, a part of the life and being of the community, but so far as men were conscious of it as being made—and we can see the beginnings of this in the ninth century, and, after a chaotic interval in the tenth century, it revived in the twelfth and thirteenth—the law was made not by any one person or assembly, but in some sense by the acceptance of the whole community. The idea of a single authorita-

tive legislator was wholly alien to the temper of the
Middle Ages.

In the second place, we must bear in mind that the
system of law was thought of as being the embodiment of
justice, and as having no authority, no validity, except in
so far as it had this character. It is true that there was
an authority against this, that of St. Augustine in his
unhappy attempt, in one part of the *De Civitate Dei,* to
eliminate the conception of justice from the theory of the
State, but, fortunately, this exercised no influence on the
political theory of the Middle Ages. Cicero's phrases, in
which he sets out the principle that law is the expression
of justice, were well known to them, partly at least
through the fact that St. Augustine had quoted them in
another chapter of the same work. It is this conception
that was drawn out most completely by the great jurists
of the revived study of the Roman law in the twelfth and
thirteenth centuries. *"Jus,"* or the whole system of law,
is the manifestation and expression of *iustitia.*

The same principle was also set out under another set
of terms especially by the canonists, that is under the
term of the relation of the law of any particular community to the "natural law." The "natural law," Gratian says, is superior to all other laws, it is primitive and
unchangeable, it is the expression of the will of God Himself; all laws or constitutions, whether ecclesiastial or
secular, which are contrary to the "natural law" are null
and void.

This is not the place for a discussion of all that was
implied in history by the conception of a natural law, as
a principle of justice, antecedent in authority to all positive or civil law; but we must take account of this, for it
meant that while mediæval people thought of law as the
custom, or sometimes as the determination of the com-

munity, they were clear that it had no authority, no validity at all unless it was the expression of something more than either custom or will.

The history of the gradual development of the theory of an absolute authority, a "sovereignty" in society, has not yet been fully studied or written, and indeed, much serious work will have to be done, before this can be attempted. It is, however, possible to recognize something of what happened.

The conception of the supremacy of law in the State was profound and just, but it is also true that it was not possible that it should continue under the older terms. It became evident that it was necessary to find a power behind the law, greater than the law, which could change the law. For some centuries men were content to modify or reinterpret custom, to adapt it to the changing conditions and requirements of life; but in the end this proved insufficient, and they had to recognize the necessity of a legislative power. We can trace the beginnings both of the process and of the theory of legislation in the twelfth and thirteenth centuries, but it was only very slowly that men became fully conscious of it, and for centuries the process concealed itself, especially in a country like England, behind the appeal to precedent. In the end, however, the facts triumphed over tradition, and men came, however slowly, to think of the law not as itself supreme but as the expression of the will of a supreme power which lay behind it. This is the meaning of that distinction between the legislative and the judical authority which has on the whole established itself as normally useful.

I am not here concerned with the various forms under which the conception has found expression. In some countries, indeed in most European countries after the fifteenth century, the supreme authority was thought to be embodied in an absolute king, in others, and especially in England, in an "omnicompetent" parliament. The difference is profound and immensely significant in history, for one represents the principle of what we justly call political slavery, the other at least the possibility of political freedom. But in spite of this immense difference, for our present purpose the distinction is not material. What we are here concerned with is the development of the notion, whether under one form or the other, that there is such a thing as an absolute sovereign power.

It is this doctrine, set out with characteristic and paradoxical vehemence by Hobbes, which is probably the most dangerous, the most mischievous foolishness of political theory. For in Hobbes this is the expression of a complete disbelief in any moral principle in society, to him the terms just and unjust are merely the euphemistic forms under which men express the sum of what is useful or convenient. To him men seek in the State not justice but safety, there is only one "right of nature" (*jus naturale*) and that is self-preservation, and that can only be secured under the protection of an absolute and unlimited power, which, for its own convenience or advantage, will normally secure the individual man from the ferocious aggressions of his fellowmen.

It is true that in this extreme form the conception of the existence of an absolute sovereignty has not been often professed, but it is also true that the theory of the safety or the convenience of society as something which is beyond right and wrong, beyond justice or injustice, has often found its expression under the terms of the theory of the absolute sovereignty of the State.

It was natural enough that a similar theory should

have found expression in the actual conditions of economic life in the eighteenth and nineteeth centuries, a
theory that human relations in the economic sphere are to
be determined not at all by the principles of justice, but
by those of convenience.   The natural consequence has
been that the characteristic aspect of the economic relations of men in the industrial world is the dominance
of force, or what is in other terms described as the "class-
war."   No doubt respectable persons pretend that this is
not their meaning or their intention, but unhappily for
them, facts are what they are, and the social condition
of Europe is a sufficient evidence of the reality.

I am not here dealing with the economic aspect of
society, but with its proper characteristic or quality under
all its forms.   And I conclude therefore by urging that
it is imperiously necessary that we should recover from
the superstition of absolute authority, and that we may
well find it useful to return to and learn something from a
time when men firmly believed that justice, and not force,
was supreme.   No doubt it is a mere absurdity to think
that we can go back, or to imagine that the immense complexities of modern life can be solved by a mere appeal to
great principles.   The task of the modern world is to
work out these principles into a system which may under
our conditions, and with relation to the necessary
movement of life, serve to embody them.

THE OBSTACLE OF INDUSTRIALISM

BY

ARTHUR J. PENTY

Author of *Post-Industrialism, Old Worlds for New*, etc.

SYNOPSIS

The disproportion that exists between the material and spiritual sides of modern life. The conflict between industrial and spiritual values. Luxury a disintegrating social influence. Leads to catastrophe. Luxury and unemployment. The quantitative standard antipathetic to Christianity. Current fallacies in economics rest on the acceptance of a false philosophy of life. Self-expression through work a spiritual necessity. Machinery and sub-division of labour. Over-specialization the bane of the modern world. Intellectual specialization. Necessity of placing a limit to specialization. Creative impulse incompatible with the sub-division of labour. Industrial system will break down of its own weight. The unemployed problem. The need of a changed conception of life. Guilds and the Just Price. The regulation of machinery. Should not be allowed to supplant craftsmanship. Dependence of design on handicraft. Art and industrialism. Opposition of quantitative and qualitative standards. Fallacy of expecting a spontaneous creation of art. How the change will come. On the teaching of taste. The Christian temper in art. Modernist and academic standards. Necessity of a religious basis for art.

CHAPTER VI

THE OBSTACLE OF INDUSTRIALISM

NOT the least of the obstacles that stand in the way of a return of Christendom is the monstrous disproportion that exists between the material and spiritual sides of life. For centuries, and especially since the Industrial Revolution, a larger and larger proportion of our energies have been devoted to the increase and development of our material resources, with the result that the balance between the material and spiritual sides of life which is indispensable to any healthy and normal civilization has been entirely destroyed, and the spiritual life almost crushed out of existence by the dead weight of material preoccupations.

The fact that undue concentration on material things tends to choke the spiritual life was over and over again insisted upon by Jesus Christ. "Take ye no thought, saying, What shall we eat, or what shall we drink, or wherewithal shall we be clothed (for after all these things do the Gentiles seek)? for your heavenly Father knoweth that ye have need of these things. But seek ye first the kingdom of God, and His righteousness, and all these things shall be added unto you." This is the true political economy; it is the political economy of Christendom, and it is because in some measure the Mediævalists pursued this ideal that they were not perplexed by the problem of riches and poverty as it perplexes us to-day. Industrialism is the organization of society on the opposite assumption, "Seek ye first," it says, "material prosperity, and all other things shall be added unto you." But somehow or other it does not work out. These other things are not added, and in the long run the pursuit of riches does not even bring material prosperity. For the concentration of all effort and mental energy upon material achievement upsets the spiritual equilibrium of society. It produces contrasts of wealth and poverty, and out of these come envy, jealousy, class hatreds, economic and military warfare, and finally the destruction of the wealth that has been so laboriously created. For no society built on a lie can endure.

Our industrial society exhibits a spirit that shows itself irreconcilably hostile to all the higher interests of mankind, and all men who care for spiritual things are conscious of this antagonism. Yet as a nation we lack the courage to face the fact that Industrialism is incompatible with the spiritual life. In the Middle Ages, when the material development of civilization was in its infancy, there were not wanting men to protest with all their might against the corrupting influence of wealth and luxury. St. Francis, in the thirteenth century even, sought to counter the evil by preaching the Gospel of Poverty, and at a later date sumptuary laws were enacted to put a boundary to the growth of personal extravagance, for many people saw the social dangers attendant upon an increase of luxury. In Germany, which in the Middle Ages was the most prosperous country in Europe, extravagance and luxury grew at an alarming pace towards the end of the fifteenth century. Many of the merchants had become richer than kings and emperors, and vanity had prompted them to give visible evidence of their great riches in the adoption of a higher and higher standard of living.

Feasting and gambling increased, while extravagance in dress became the order of the day. Commenting on this, Wimpheling, who was one of the most widely read authors of the period, said that "wealth and prosperity are attended with great dangers, as we see exemplified: they induce extravagance in dress, in banqueting, and what is still worse, they engender a desire for still more. This desire debases the mind of man and degenerates into contempt of God, His Church, and His Commandments." And experience was to prove it led to social catastrophe.

The peril arises from the fact that, as extravagance increases, a kind of social compulsion is brought to bear upon others to live up to it whether they can afford to do so or not, and as only the rich can afford to keep up with the standard thus set, a point is soon reached when the need of money is very widely felt. When that point was reached in Germany the same thing happened that has happened with us to-day. Nobody wanted to do any really productive work, but everybody wanted to go into trade where money was to be made. Mercantile houses, shops, and taverns multiplied inordinately, and complaints were made that there was no money but only debts, and that whole districts were drained by usury. The growth of this state of things was followed by the attempt which each class made to save itself from bankruptcy by transferring its burdens on to the shoulders of the class beneath it, which led to the progressive impoverishment of the working class, who had to bear the brunt because the burden could be shifted no farther. Then there arose a bitter enmity between the propertied and the unpropertied classes, and class hatred increased in intensity until finally it led in 1524 to the Peasants' War, which convulsed almost every corner of the Empire from the Alps to the Baltic.

We see then that in attacking extravagance and luxury the Church has been led by a true social instinct. But it becomes daily more evident that to attack extravagance and luxury is not enough. It is necessary to attack those general principles and assumptions of our social and industrial system which of their own nature tend to promote such vices. This fact has of late received some recognition by the Church. The Report of the Archbishop's Committee on "Christianity and Industrial Problems" marks an advance in thought to the extent that it has broken away from that purely personal explanation of social phenomena which satisfied most Churchmen until yesterday, and has recognized that "charity" with the Church has not been interpreted (as it should be) as "a sort of glorified justice" that "looks at least as much to the prevention of evil as to its cure. On the contrary, it has meant far too exclusively what may be called ambulance work for mankind—the picking up of the wounded and the curing of their wounds." "We have," says the Report, "neglected to attack the forces of wrong. We have been content with the ambulance work when we ought to have been assaulting the strongholds of evil."

In laying down the broad principles which should govern the conduct of Christians in their relation to social questions nothing could be more admirable than this Report. But as it proceeds, the clear vision that marks the early part of the Report gets bedimmed and the writers get entangled in the economic defences of the existing system. Their protests are silenced by those pleas of economic necessity behind which the upholders of the existing order take cover. Thus while on the one hand luxury is attacked, on the other the Report hesitates to carry its attack to its logical conclusion by condemning root and branch those quantitative conceptions upon which our industrial system is based. For it is undoubtedly true that the progressive growth of luxury is a necessary condition of the continued existence of a system that is based upon conceptions of indefinite industrial expansion. It is not too much to say that people nowadays are goaded by advertisers into becoming luxurious. Indeed, unless a man is poor, his difficulty nowadays is how to avoid becoming luxurious, for circumstances combine to force the individual along the path of luxury whether he likes it or not, and people succumb to luxurious tendencies because they are afraid to appear mean. It may be admitted that expenditure need not be luxurious though it pass the bounds of necessity. Expenditure on the arts, for instance, is of this nature. But this is not the kind of expenditure that is encouraged by latter-day conceptions of industrial expansion. On the contrary, what is encouraged in every sort of vain and useless expenditure on all kinds of things that people would be better without; while the dilemma in which we are placed is that such useless expenditure is necessary to keep the wheels of industry running. There is plenty of unemployment to-day, yet under our existing system if the rich could be induced to abandon luxury unemployment would be actually increased. Hence it is that until we have the courage to attack the principles upon which the industrial system is built there can be no escape from this fundamental dilemma.

This kind of inconsistency must come to an end. We must frankly recognize that the purely quantitative standard is antipathetic to everything that Christianity stands for, for not until we do shall we be able to translate our ideals into the terms of actuality. We must oppose the conception of "maximum production" with that of a "sufficient production." Quantity up to a certain point of course we must have, but we must break with the theory that exalts a standard of quantity as the final test of industrial righteousness, since so long as we accept such a standard, the time will never come when we can say we have produced enough. Appearances will always be against a return to sanity, because when production proceeds beyond a certain point it upsets distribution; and by upsetting distribution, competition is increased and unemployment and poverty is created. The widespread existence of such poverty in turn lends a colour to the demand for still more production, and so we go on from bad to worse, driven from one desperate expedient to another in a vain effort to escape from the consequences of exalting the quantitative standard. The remedy is for us to refuse any longer to sacrifice Christian principles to economic expediency. We can be perfectly assured that what is wrong morally is bad economics; and that professors of economics who maintain the contrary suffer from a constitutional inability to distinguish between appearance and reality.

When we search for an explanation of current fallacies of economics we find that they rest finally on a false philosophy of life—on the belief that work at the best is a disagreeable necessity that it is desirable to reduce to a minimum. In former times it was the normal thing for men to find pleasure and satisfaction in their work. But this is no longer the case. The vast majority of people to-day do not look for any such pleasure or satisfaction. They work in order to get money to live. Their hearts are not in their work, their real interests are outside, either in the pursuit of pleasure, or in some hobby or occupation extraneous to their daily work. Not only do they do as little as they can, but what they do is done in a venal and slovenly way. The grudging and resentful temper engendered by their daily work infects the whole of life. Character deterioriates: men become restless and dissatisfied. It would matter little if the hours of work were reduced to four or even two hours a day. They would still be restless and dissatisfied. For they would still be in a fundamentally wrong relation to life, and that fact would vitiate the extra leisure they had gained. Men are not men until they have found their true vocation and ministry. When Carlyle said, "Blessed is the man who has found his work: let him ask no other blessedness," he was expressing one of the primary truths of Christian ethics.

All Christians must deplore this demoralization that has overtaken the modern world, and many Christian moralists, recognizing the evil, have attempted to combat it. But they have all failed. They have failed to establish points of contact with the modern mind, and this for the simple reason that they have chosen to ignore the vital facts of the situation. With men to-day as in the past it would be the normal and natural thing for them to find pleasure in their work were it not that they are prevented from doing so by circumstances. Their work fails to inspire them for two reasons. Firstly because as it is done at the dictation and in the interests of profiteers, they cannot feel the call of service; and secondly, because under our industrial system work has become so monotonous that everyone is bored by it.

Recognizing these facts, any analysis of the problem of work and industry that would grapple with the realities of the situation must reassert the claims of the producer. It may be true that the needs of the consumer are the primary basis of any economic system. Yet the producer has equal claims for consideration, since an analysis based entirely upon the needs of the consumer will, if carried to its logical conclusion, lead inevitably to the enslavement and degradation of the producer, for instead of being regarded as a human being he will come to be regarded merely as an instrument for the increase of wealth. To such an extent has development proceeded in this direction that the only way to restore a condition of normality in industry is to assert the claims of the producer, affirming self-expression through work to be a spiritual necessity. The moment we assert this we come into collision with Industrialism as a machine producing wealth, no matter how equitably its products could under some future system be distributed, because it denies all opportunities whatsoever for self-expression.

Industrialism destroys interest in work because it tends towards an ever increasing specialization. This is the key to the problem. We are accustomed to associate the evil with the spread of machine production, but strictly speaking the evil does not reside in machinery, but in the subdivision of labour which preceded the introduction of machinery and which is responsible for its misapplication. And here it is necessary to distinguish between the division of labour which is legitimate and the subdivision of labour which is illegitimate. The former is a necessity in every civilized community, for it is obvious that a man cannot supply all his own needs, since to some extent he is inevitably dependent upon others. No sooner did civilization begin to develop than this necessity brought about the specialization of men into different trades. One man became a weaver, another a carpenter, and so forth. Up to this point the division of labour is justified, not merely because it is a necessity of civilization, but because it enlarges the opportunities of expression of the individual. What, however, we understand by the subdivision of labour is measures taken to increase the output in the interests of profiteering by splitting up a trade into a great number of separate processes. This we must condemn, because by reducing men to autom- atons it undermines their moral and spiritual life and distintegrates personality, while it leads inevitably to sweating and economic insecurity. This system came into existence in the early part of the seventeenth century, the classical example being that eulogized by Adam Smith in *The Wealth of Nations,* namely pin-making, in which industry, he explained, it takes twenty men to make a pin, each man being specialized on a single process for a life- time. In our day this method has reached its logical con- clusion in the system known as "scientific management." The subdivision of labour attacks the craft; scientific management attacks the man. Its acknowledged object is further to increase output by the elimination of all the motions of the arms and fingers and body that do not directly contribute to the fashioning of the article under process of manufacture. As such it completes the de- humanization and despiritualization of labour begun by the subdivision of labour.

Now it is apparent that the value to be placed upon such a method of work will depend upon our philosophy of life. If we are materialists and are convinced that the great end of life is to increase wealth—profit and com- modities—regardless of the use to which the commodities are put or the degradation of the workers through the methods employed in their production, then we shall regard even such a system as scientific management as evidence of progress. But if we believe as Christians in the aboriginal and imperishable worth of the individual, we shall condemn the system as essentially anti-Christian. We shall maintain that any increase of wealth obtained by such means carries with it a curse, inasmuch as it ignores the sacredness of human personality and degrades man to the level of a machine.

The principle of the subdivision of labour has penetrated into every department of human activity. Over-specialization is the bane of the modern world. It affects the intellectual world, not perhaps to the same degree, but with results that are as potent for evil as those which we deplore in the world of labour. For just as the machine-tender becomes atrophied in certain directions, so the intellectual specialist develops one side of his mind at the expense of other sides, and thereby loses that balance and judgment which are essential to work of permanent value. It is said that in Germany before the War specialization among intellectual workers had reached such a degree of development that men tended to become monomaniacs on one subject, or even one small part of a subject, to the detriment of general culture. This was the Kultur that gave to the Germans their sense of superiority over other peoples and was a contributory cause of the War. Specialization up to a certain point we must have if civilization is to exist at all. But a limit must be placed somewhere if men are not to disintegrate morally, intellectually, and spiritually, and to imperil the stability of civilization. An intimate connection exists between the convulsions which have overtaken society and this over-specialization; since when specialization is complete it breaks up society, because the co-ordinating idea which binds men together no longer operates. It is the corollary of that isolation of the soul which Mr. Belloc rightly sees as the fruit of the Reformation.

I said that to the development of specialization a limit must be placed somewhere. That limit, I submit, should be placed at the point craft development had reached before the division of labour degenerated into the sub-division of labour. To suffer specialization to proceed farther is, to use an engineering term "to trespass on the margin of safety." In calculating the strengths of the material he uses, the engineer keeps well within the margin of safety, for he knows that all structures suffer from wear and tear and may at some time or other be subjected to an exceptional strain, and therefore in common prudence he makes allowances for such contin-gencies in his calculations, distinguishing clearly between a "safe load" and a "breaking load." A sane sociology would make a corresponding destruction. It would recognize that there was a limit beyond which produc-tivity could not be increased without imperilling the stability of the social structure. It would condemn the subdivision of labour because it trespassed on the margin of psychological safety and indefinite industrial expan-sion because it trespassed on the margin of economic safety. Failure to recognize the truth of this principle is responsible for the disintegration of society to-day. Though it is only since the War that our peril has received any public recognition, the process of disinte-gration has nevertheless been at work since the seven-teenth century, when the subdivision of labour was insti-tuted. If, then, society is to be reconstructed on a stable basis, productivity must not be allowed to trespass on the margin of safety; in other words, we must repudiate the subdivision of labour and return to the handicrafts as the basis of production, using machinery only in an accessory way.

It is now some seventy years since Ruskin wrote his impassioned protests against the human degradation involved in the subdivision of labour. Yet it is only of late that any signs have been forthcoming that his protests have not been entirely in vain. Thus in the Report of the American Committee on "The Church and Industrial Reconstruction" we read: "The tendency to regard labour simply as a means of production has been greatly intensified by modern machinery which has often had the effect of reducing the man almost to the level of a machine. He is left to do what inventive genius is unable to design a machine to do. The process of manufacture is carried to a higher and higher degree of specialization, until the worker's task tends to become a deadening routine and he himself hardly more than a semi-mechanical part of the factory. These conditions almost inevitably result in the loss of the sense of personal creation and fine craftsmanship. In the simpler days before the advent of large-scale production the worker helped to plan the work and with his own strength and skill to carry it into execution. In such a task a man could really find self-expression. But now he does not plan the work or any part of it, and everything except the monotonous details is accomplished by an automatic machine. The work no longer seems really his. The factory, therefore, means barren monotony for millions of men, deadens their imagination, and robs them of any sense of creative joy, and in these results we have had an altogether too complacent acquiescence. If we are seriously concerned about the development of personality we ought to be earnestly seeking ways of affording to modern workers opportunity for self-expression in their tasks by giving them industrial education and making it possible for them to share in directing the industry as a whole. At the very least we ought to guarantee them sufficient leisure for self-development in other activities outside the factory. We have shown an inexcusable apathy towards this destruction of human values in the process of producing things. We have been concerned with impersonal goods, with profits and dividends, forgetting that the factor we indifferently spoke of as 'labour' is nothing less than immortal souls for whom the Lord Christ died."[1]

Well, it is something to get an acknowledgment of the problem, but the measures proposed in the report will not, I fear, get us anywhere, for the real issues are not faced. The writers of the Report see our industrial system as an established fact, and they are cowed and overawed by it much in the same way that dwellers in tropical latitudes are said to be cowed and overawed by the stupendous nature they see around them. And so instead of facing the issue, instead of frankly recognizing the fact that a system of industry that is built upon the degradation of the workers must be abolished, they seek to evade the dilemma in the typical modern fashion by recommending palliatives which experience should already have taught us effect nothing.

If one may take the Selected Bibliography attached to this volume as indicating the lines on which its authors think industrial reform should proceed, the idea apparently is to salute Henry Ford as a prophet; and to seek an escape from the evil of over-specialization, not by its abolition, but by constantly changing the workers round, so that instead of condemning them for a lifetime to the performance of a single task they would move from one specialism to another, and to supplement such experience by a scheme of technical education which will enable them to see the thing as a whole. By such means we are told the creative impulse will be restored to industry, and all will be well. The idea is meeting with

[1] Pp. 38-39.

much support as may well be imagined, for all ideas which do not demand of us real sacrifices are popular until their inadequacy is found out.

Still it won't do. The creative impulse in man will not be liberated by such means any more than a man would be liberated from prison because he enjoyed the privilege of being moved from cell to cell. And for this reason, that the element of choice as to how anything should be done would be entirely missing, and liberty of choice is an indispensable accompaniment of the exercise of the creative impulse. Hence we see that any such compromise does not really change the problem, and that the liberation of the creative impulse is incompatible with the existence of the subdivision of labour.

The difficulty of securing acceptance for a truth that is self-evident to men with experience is due to the fact that so few writers have any industrial experience to build upon. As the effects of the system spread and begin to alter their own lives they become in an indirect way conscious of the fact that the industrial system suppresses creative instincts within themselves and so they rebel. But what is the nature of such instincts and what is the kind of industrial conditions favourable to their expression they have no notion whatsoever, and being therefore without any positive experience they hesitate to challenge such an established fact as the industrial system. The tragedy of the situation, however, is that while owing to lack of experience they do not know the truth themselves, they are unwilling to accept the opinion of craftsmen and artists who having had experience have some right to be heard. Meanwhile the industrial system proceeds according to the laws of its own being regardless of consequences. The few skilled men necessary to its continuance are rapidly disappearing, and as the system trains no successors it is clear that the day is not far distant when there will be no competence left to run it. It will not be long before the system breaks down of its own weight.

So much may be seen clearly as the logical consequence of the persistent refusal of the modern world to listen to the advice of anyone who has had real experience of the problem. If we are to learn at all it would seem it can only be through suffering. Our statesmen and publicists have for centuries refused to look facts in the face. They have lived on the principle of putting off the evil day, and now it can be put off no longer. The unemployed are in our streets, and I venture to say they will remain there until the facts are faced. Our markets are contracting and will remain contracted, for during the War many of our former customers have taken to manufacturing all kinds of things for themselves because we could not supply their needs, and they will continue to do so. Meanwhile automatic machinery is being introduced into industry after industry and the workers are beginning to realize that there is such a thing as a problem of machinery. The men who are unemployed are beginning to talk about it. They see that if with contracted markets more machinery is to be used there is no chance of them ever getting back to work. The newspapers have not laid bare this aspect of the subject yet, and it is to be presumed that the facts will not be faced until the last quack remedy has been tried.

My belief that the present industrial system will be transformed is not then based upon any expectation that the majority of men will so long as they can avoid doing so demand change, but on the conviction that as the present system is becoming rapidly unworkable we must

change or perish.   Meanwhile, if a nucleus of clear
thinking could be created, when the crisis does arrive
there would be something around which thought and
activity could crystallize, and in this connection it is to
be observed that nothing is any use at all that does not
go down to fundamentals.   The present system with all
its evils rests finally on a certain conception of life, on
the idea that a life of leisure and luxury is the thing
to be aimed at.   It is the general prevalence of this ideal
that is responsible for the race for wealth and the misapplication of machinery, which naturally flows from it.
When we realize these things, we realize that any reform
to be effective demands as its accompaniment a changed
ideal of life.   It means that the ideal of leisure be supplanted by one of work and service on a basis of function.
The implications of such a changed ideal of life are
simply enormous.   It would mean in the first place that
occupations would not be esteemed in proportion as they
win money, afford comfort and leisure, and confer individual power and distinction, but in proportion as they
afford the individual the opportunity of doing work that
is useful and desirable for the purposes of human life.
It would mean that instead of trade and commerce being
exalted at the expense of agriculture and the productive arts, agriculture and craftsmanship would come to
be exalted in the future as in the past as the foundation
of national prosperity and well-being, and measures
would be taken to protect all such workers against their
position being undermined by speculators in finance by
the maintenance of a Just and Fixed Price under a
system of Guilds covering the whole of society.

In addition it would be necessary to regulate machinery, in the first place, because there can be no economic
security for the worker so long as his means of liveli-

hood is at the mercy of a new invention; and in the next, because it is an essential condition of any decent and stable social order that machinery be brought into subjection by the abolition of all machinery that involves the subdivision of labour, and this necessitates regulation. Moralists who affirm that no such regulation is required, inasmuch as machinery is non-moral and therefore its application will be good or bad according to the motive that inspires its use, should, to be consistent, deny the necessity of laws and regulations in every other department of activity, since the case for regulating machinery rests finally on precisely the same grounds as any other kind of regulation: First, to restrain those whose motives are bad from injuring society by their actions, and, secondly, to prevent those who with the best of motives do things through ignorance which in their ultimate effects are harmful.

If these principles were observed, the amount of machinery used in the future would be negligible in comparison with what is used to-day, and it would so obviously be performing the function which it professes to perform that no case could be made out against its use. This would mean that machinery would not be allowed to trespass on the domain of the crafts, but its use would be confined to doing the "donkey work" which lies at the base of production. The point at which its use would be forbidden would be where a man has to think more about the machinery than the work he is doing, and where those directing industry have to think more about how they are to keep their plant running than of the service which their activities render to the community. The application of this principle, however, involves other things. It presupposes that simultaneously efforts are made to restore the Guilds, and to reestablish communal traditions of art and craftsmanship, since apart from the positive values that such traditions would give the problem of exactly where to draw the line could not be easily determined.

At this point we find ourselves drawn into the controversies that surround the revival of the arts. Twenty years ago all who were interested in the subject would have agreed that the re-establishment of any such traditions was dependent upon a revival of handicraft. Following Ruskin and Morris, they would have affirmed that there is no such thing as art apart from handicraft, inasmuch as any new ideas in design arise from experimental handicraft, just, I might add, in the same way that new ideas in science are discovered by similarly experimenting with material. But of late years, owing to the failure of the Arts and Craft Movement to solve the economic problems in which it found itself involved, attempts have been made to adjust art to the requirements of machine industry. All such compromisers would I believe admit that at the best such machine art was on a distinctly lower plane than that of handicraft. But seeing no option in the matter, the Design and Industries Association was organized to make the best of a bad job by bringing art into relation to modern industry. It is interesting to note that their experience has been equally disappointing. Like the Arts and Crafts, they have here and there been able to make a little headway. They have been able to get a few utilitarian things of better design on the market, but there is no denying that they have failed as miserably as the Arts and Crafts Movement to reform industrialism, which as a whole exhibits a spirit entirely antagonistic to any change in an artistic direction, and this is no wonder, for the demands of art and industrialism are mutually exclusive. Thus the most fundamental requirement of the growth of any new tradition of art is continuity of effort in a certain given direction. A tradition is a growth, and it becomes full and rich in its capacities of expression through work along certain continuous lines. But industrialism denies this condition. Its interest in output forbids it to work with continuity. On the contrary it seeks to create new demand by constantly changing the fashion. Change of fashion, it will be seen, means that every year the basis is changed, and therefore there is no continuity and therefore no growth. In the same way a hundred other interests militate against a growth of tradition. Such experiences drive us inevitably to the conclusion that a quantitative standard and a qualitative standard are opposed and that finally no compromise is possible between them.

Yet people are unwilling to admit this, for to admit it seems to most people a gospel of sheer despair. Hence it has happened, partly as a result of these failures, and partly as a misunderstanding as to the democratic nature of art, that of late years the theory has been advanced that the revival of art is not to come from professional artists and craftsmen—that is from the people who think about it, but from the masses who don't—whose creative impulse will find spontaneous expression when they are liberated from economic servitude. Needless to say, no one holds this theory who has any capacity for æsthetic production himself. Nevertheless it is widely held by people who are interested but without experience, and as these people, if they only knew it, really hold the key to the situation, it is important that it be controverted.

Let us suppose then that the people were liberated from economic servitude. What kind of work would

they produce? Well, I think we may take it for granted
that they would not produce shoddy and scamped work;
but I think I am safe in saying that if left to themselves they would (so far as the æsthetic side of their
work is concerned) continue to produce very much the
same kind of thing they make to-day, and this for the
simple reason that to produce anything different they
would need to be born again æsthetically and spiritually.
Economic emancipation would not of itself do this for
them.

Whatever illusions we may harbour as to the possibility of a spontaneous democratic creation of art are
speedily dissipated when we talk to the average man;
we have not to talk to him long to discover that he recognizes no ultimate standards of thought or taste. One
man likes this, and another likes that, and that is the
end of it, for there is no accounting for tastes. The
idea that he cannot get hold of is that there is a right
and wrong in questions of taste as in other matters, and
because he cannot get hold of it he must remain where
he is or follow the lead of others, for he is incapable
of leadership himself. And if the individual does not
thus possess within himself the perception that would
emancipate him, we can be sure the masses will not, for
in their collective capacity the tyranny of majorities
tends inevitably to maintain the *status quo*. Thus we
are led to see that any revival of art does not depend
upon mass action, but upon individuals whose æsthetic
perceptions are such as to enable them to lead the way—
that is by the gradual enlargement of the circle of people
who nowadays have some idea of what they are about.
As this circle widens, art becomes democratic because
it becomes generalized and provides a medium of expression in which all may share. Thus we see that in

affirming that art shall be democratic we do not mean that we look forward to a time when a new form of æsthetic expression will arise spontaneously out of the whims and fancies of undisciplined tastes, but that the nature of the art we seek to promote shall be such as to be capable of popular understanding and incorporation. In a word, it is a conception of æsthetic activity that proceeds to the people seeking their regeneration, not a gospel of despair demanding that the uneducated shall save the educated.

Evidence is not wanting that the change is coming in this way. We speak of the failure of the Arts and Crafts Movement and in the sense that those actively engaged in it have not done what they hoped to do, it is true. Yet it has not entirely failed. The improvement that has taken place in the democratic arts of house furnishing and ladies' dress during the last twenty or thirty years, for example, amounts to a revolution. Yet, I venture to say, it is largely the consequence of the work of Morris and the Arts and Crafts Movement. This movement goes on underground, unobserved by art critics. True it has a long way to go yet. Still it has got a good start. Twenty years ago it was rare to find the house of an educated person furnished with any taste. Nowadays it is just as rare to go into one that does not exhibit some. From them it will percolate down until all are affected, once the economic barriers are removed.

There is no greater illusion in this world than to imagine that taste cannot be taught. Of course it is impossible to teach it to anyone who has not something within himself that will respond to the suggestions of the teacher, but granted that something is there (and in a greater or lesser degree most people have some inherent æsthetic sensibility), then taste can certainly be taught. It will develop in all such people if they are in personal contact with others in whom it is developed. I remember how this was brought home to me some twenty-five years ago. I used to imagine that I had no taste in colour, till one day I went round the National Gallery with a painter who gave me his opinion as to the merits of pictures there. He told me that this was good colour and that was bad; at the time I could not understand the reasons that led him to bestow his praise and blame. I listened to what he had to say and said little myself, and some time later it gradually dawned upon me what he meant. Afterwards a time came when I could discriminate with as much confidence as he did.

This brings me to what is a very crucial issue. The great difficulty connected with the teaching of taste is that most people resent criticism. They resent the dogmatism of the artist as something which if admitted would crush them. But this is an illusion, for if they only knew it, submission to such dogmatism would liberate them. To learn in art, as in other things, depends upon a certain humility of temper which allows a man to subordinate himself to anyone whom he feels knows more about anything than himself. If he will do this, a time comes when he will grow out of his pupilage and begin to feel his own feet. But too few will be content to act so, their pride seems to stand in the way. They want to run before they can walk. Yet everything depends upon the cultivation of such a temper. Pride is as great an enemy of art as of life.

Such considerations enforce the conclusion that while a solution of the economic problem is an indispensable condition of the triumph of art in the world, yet its revival is not ultimately dependent upon a solution of such difficulties, but upon the cultivation of a certain temper or attitude of mind—a temper and attitude which may be described as Christian. It goes with a certain respect for mastership and a capacity for subordinating oneself to a master, while it is frustrated by the prevailing temper of self-assertion, both among artist whose pride leads them to desire to be thought original, and with the man-in-the-street who "knows what he likes" and has no desire to learn. The truth is that all great masters have been willing learners, while their dogmatism does not arise from egotism and pride, but from the self-confidence that follows patient study—the knowledge that they understand certain things and their desire for others to share in their knowledge. The great artist always begins by subordinating himself to the needs of a communal tradition and ends by transcending it. The minor artist will not submit himself to such a discipline. He suffers from an anxiety to preserve his own individuality and therefore fails to achieve distinction in anything. He that would save his life must lose it, is a truth for the artist as much as for the saint.

I said that a great artist subordinates himself to the needs of a great tradition, as such his spirit is democratic, for the true democratic spirit does not seek to give the public merely what it wants, but seeks rather to subordinate itself to what the public needs—two very different things. In the world of to-day, however, there is no established communal tradition of art. To what then does he subordinate himself? To the communal traditions of the past. Not in any dead antiquarian sense, but as a source of living inspiration; for to those living in an age in which there is no established tradition of art, the past is the ultimate source of inspiration. Even the modernist schools in their rebellion against academic standards do not really rebel against the past, but against a particular interpretation or valuation of the past, for their difference from the academic school is only that in their search for a source of inspiration they go much farther back. The academists held up the later phase of Greek and Gothic art as models to be followed, the modernists on the contrary take the more primitive forms of Greek and Gothic art as a source of inspiration. At any rate the best of them do. Those who seek to cut themselves off from the past altogether merely become eccentric.

Meanwhile the whole trend of social and economic development is to thrust art entirely out of society. What little art we have with us to-day is bound up with the old social order that is fast disappearing—whether it will disappear completely remains to be seen. But there is no doubt whatsoever that it is being crushed out of existence between the upper and nether millstones of plutocracy and industrialism, for experience proves art is incompatible with both and all efforts to graft art on modern civilization can only fail in the end. Hence the conviction grows that the only hope for art in the world is to get back to its old basis in religion, from which all the great traditions of art in the past have derived. It may well be that if our aspirations were fulfilled and a new Christendom should return, that art would recover its place in society in fuller measure and more complete perfection.

THE MORALIZATION OF PROPERTY

BY

MAURICE B. RECKITT, M.A.

SYNOPSIS

I

The Christian claim necessarily involves not only the salvation of the individual, but the resurrection of society. The failure of Christians themselves to realize this has largely accounted for the ineffectiveness of their witness. For the Faith thus never appears to the world in the light of a unique clue to its problems.

Yet the world is waiting precisely for such a clue, and to a large extent consciously so. It realizes its need of social salvation, but many of its best spirits have despaired of the most fundamental institutions of society in view of the seemingly fatal corruptions which have overtaken them. Especially have they despaired of the institution of property.

That institution is still defended by arguments totally inapplicable to it as at present distorted by plutocracy. But plutocracy cares nothing for property, save as a means to the establishment of monopoly, for it is at monopoly essentially which plutocracy aims. There is a case for property, however, which the exposure of its abuses to-day can only strengthen.

II

The ideal of Christendom is in no way Utopian, but one of immediate and practical significance. It offers in particular a clue to the problem of Property by the achievement of harmony between personal freedom and social function.

While a clue, however, cannot in itself resolve all difficulties, it gives us ground for confidence in facing them. We may gain assurance in this instance that property-holding offers opportunities which are a necessary part of the vocation of the average Christian, while the obligations of fraternity must determine the conditions in which they are exercised.

Property has been distorted by private monopoly owing to the idea that liberty being a purely individual right, property rights were consequently absolute, neither being related to any social purpose. A reaction from these errors leads many to propose replacing private monopolies by public ones—a development equally perilous to social freedom.

But it is certain that no solution can be found in the evolution of plutocracy. For this develops property rights only as a means to power, and leads to the domination of society by the power of money, an influence totally incompatible with brotherhood. This influence breeds recklessness both in the wealthy and in the destitute, while it creates in the middle class only a spiritless timidity.

III

The socialist doctrine has a superficial cogency. But it raises immediately many wide questions relating to property-holding on which Socialists themselves in nowise agree. Two main schools of thought, however, may be discerned.

(a) *Communism* is a term to which recent events have given an increased practical significance. The Russian experiment has involved the most complete attempt to extinguish property-rights ever made. But the attempt has failed because it made provision for no alternative inducements to replace those which it suppressed. Its result was but to concentrate all the tyrannies of irresponsible private property in a single body.

(b) *Collectivism,* though its adherents are critical of Communist methods, embodies a programme not greatly different in aim. It professes only to challenge property in so far as it forms part of "the means of production, distribution, and exchange." But this is a very wide definition. Before we can accept it, we have to inquire whether its application may not involve for the masses the continued deprivation of powers and opportunities which are necessary to a full citizenship.

The essence of ownership does not lie in any of the abuses to which it is subject, but in the assurance of security, the sense of responsibility, and the opportunity of choice. Without a guaranteed economic resource independent of State interference for every citizen, public monopoly leaves the individual at the mercy of the political authorities.

IV

The moralization of property involves more than recognition of their obligations on the part of the holders of existing property rights; it involves a new outlook upon the sanctions by which such rights exist. This is called for, not only in principle but for practical reasons, since *within the existing* system a new status for the worker and a new orientation of industry are impossible.

Nor can Christians find a justification for the possession and administration of great riches by taking refuge in a doctrine of "stewardship," a doctrine which contains not only spiritual falsehood but an economic fallacy.

Such an outlook upon property, moreover, finds no sanction in the Gospels. Christ, in coming "to fulfill the Law and the Prophets," endorsed both the most determined attempt to achieve the moralization of property ever made by an organized community and the protests made by the prophets against failures to preserve it. Further, in His central doctrine of the Kingdom of God He indicated that only in a community of fellowship and justice can material problems be solved.

At two epochs in history has the attitude of the Church to property been of crucial importance—in the fourth century and in the later Middle Ages. The first of these two supreme opportunities was largely thrown away, and a lack of moral initiative on the part of the Church left "the social order unadjusted to the full spirit of the Gospel."

V

Despite the first great failure of the Church, from which it has never wholly recovered, the mediæval Church did make a noble effort to develop a body of teaching which should cover every aspect of man's social life. It involved a theory of property which found its most characteristic exposition in the teaching of Aquinas, who refused to recognize any private *right* in property, and defended private property-holding on grounds essentially social. Moreover, his defence had relevance only to a social order in which a share in property was a universal experience, as was generally the case in the Middle Ages.

Mediæval economic teaching was employed as an aid to the maintenance of human solidarity, not as a dis-solvent of it. A universal social ethic was possible because of the acceptance of a common Faith. Personal responsibility was enforced not as a merely individual obligation, but in relation to a comprehensive social ideal.

It is only with reference to this ideal that the practical exemplifications of mediævalism can be understood. These, indeed, display very different ideas as to property rights from those now prevalent. The guild system, for instance, only allowed of property within the governing principles of Vocation and Fraternity, as is shown by the institution of the Just Price and the circumstances of the worker's employment. In the countryside the status of the peasant was not a proletarian one, but rather that of a partner in an agrarian co-operative association.

Mediæval thought esteemed industry, commerce, and finance in inverse ratio to that in which power belongs to them to-day. The exaltation of Labour led to the perfection of craftsmanship; avarice in trading was condemned, and usury as a means of livelihood denounced. But it was the development of finance which, by bewildering and confusing mediæval teachers, assisted to break up the moral basis of the mediæval economy. The use of money as "capital" led to efforts to found a distinction between usury and justifiable interest. Practical sanction for the latter lay in the increasing need for credit, which no social organization could adequately furnish. The problem, which proved too much for mediæval society, is in important respects similar to that which confronts our own.

VI

Mediæval conceptions of property have been dealt with because they illuminate the strength and the limitations of the Christendom ideal so far as it was grasped by the Middle Ages. Criticisms of mediæval social achievements are often beside the point in failing to recognize the value of the very attempt to formulate and maintain a moral basis for economic activities—such an attempt being an indispensable prelude to the attainment of justice and stability.

A similar attempt is demanded to-day, and the Church in formulating it would come to the rescue of the world. For want of it men are confused, and many among the "middle classes" cling to property (so far as they have experience of it) with a merely instinctive and indiscriminating tenacity which plays into the hands of the forces of plutocracy. The definition of property is stretched to include many anti-social prerogatives, most dangerous amongst which is the organized avarice of financial power, which holds sway since its claims and assumptions are generally accepted without their disasterous effects being understood.

Behind the problem of property lies the problem of credit. But whereas real credit is essentially communal and based upon the ability of the community to produce what it needs, the issue of credit to-day is outside any sort of communal control and based merely on financial considerations. The issue of credit is equivalent to the issue of money, and those who control it are in command of the most extreme manifestation of property rights arising from monopoly which plutocracy displays. The inter-action of the banks and the industrial trusts in joint control of credit-issue and price-fixing is the means whereby the community, which might be free and prosperous, is impoverished and enslaved.

VII

The implications of the public monopoly of all economic functions, as plainly stated by such a unique authority as Lenin, are wholly incompatible with the social values inherent in the Christendom ideal. Equally, the moralization of property is impossible without the repudiation of the existing economic system.

The Christendom ideal requires that in property for *use* every citizen should have a share, while property for *power* should be transmuted into communal functions regulated according to defined principles. Credit-issue and price regulation being withdrawn from plutocracy and provided for by communal processes, property loses its anti-social potentialities.

The further problem arises of relating the right of the individual to a share in the common inheritance to the facts of social production on a co-operative basis. This problem the "Distributivist" has tended to neglect. A clue to its solution lies in recognition of the fact that "the dividend is the logical successor of the wage." The distinction between a dividend and any sort of "pay" is a vital one; and the dividend has no necessary relation to "production for profit." Immediate steps towards the attainment by the individual of a share in the communal product might be taken by the establishment in well organized industries of Credit Banks based on the credit inherent in Labour's ability to produce. Such banks would afford to the workers concerned the opportunity to develop an encroaching economic control over the industry involved, ending logically in proprietorship, but not including price-fixing.

Credit Banks would further provide an economic basis for the revival of guild organization. Such a revival is indispensable to industrial self-government, and would contribute to the moralization of property by giving both the opportunity and the motive for good craftsmanship. The economic freedom involved in a share both in property and in guild organization would lead men to glorify God not only with their lips but by their acts, and translate Christendom from aspiration into reality.

CHAPTER VII

THE MORALIZATION OF PROPERTY

I

THE Christian who declares that there is no name under
heaven, save only that of his Master, through which men
may find their rescue and their hope, their vast opportunities preserved and their true natures fulfilled, is claiming
something more far-reaching than he is himself ready in
most instances to appreciate. He is preaching not only,
the redemption of personality; he is pointing to the resurrection of society. The two are as inseparable and as
interdependent in the fully comprehended Christian ideal
as they would reveal themselves to be in the completely
realized Kingdom of God upon earth. Yet the failure
of the Christian witness in the world has been largely
due to the readiness of its disciples to urge their fellow-
men to "find Christ" without any effort to reveal to them
that thus they may find Christendom. Christianity so
presented affirms indeed the soul to be precious; yet for
all that, it leaves personality frustrated and isolated. It
may lead men to hunger and thirst after righteousness,
but it tempts them to rest content with a purely subjective
realization of it. Hence the impression which remains
with the world outside that Christians, in proclaiming
"salvation," assert nothing but the possession of a kind
of spiritual patent-right, the privileges of which they are
prepared to concede, but on their own terms. The Faith

thus never appears as a clue to the problems which bewilder and terrify mankind, but merely as a drug by which the weak may hope to gain some degree of oblivion to them.

It is for a clue, however, that the world is waiting—a world, moreover, more ready to-day than it has been for many decades to realize how literally it needs to be saved; saved from the fatal consequences to which, by its worship of false values, it now finds itself irresistibly driven. Pride, avarice, contempt for brotherhood and freedom—these things have distorted the institutions through which men should find the security, the happiness, and the wide opportunities to afford them which is the very purpose of society. So far, indeed, has this process gone, that these institutions, normal to mankind in some form or another through centuries of social development, seem now diseased beyond recovery; reformers despair of them, and resort to the devising of ingenious contrivances whereby they may be effectively superceded. Dismayed by the abuses which these institutions appear increasingly to display, some despair of marriage; some of the family; others, again, of the national grouping; a few even despair of all established political forms. Most of all have those who contend for social change despaired of the institution of property. That distortion of its nature and purpose by plutocracy, to which brief reference has been made in an earlier chapter, has for many obscured by now every justification of it. They are impatient of any plea on its behalf. It is for them a mere abuse of power, an instrument of tyranny—let it go the way of all such.

It is often assumed that the defense of an institution will include a defence of its abuses: more commonly, however, it will rather involve the exposure of them.

The defence of contemporary property rights *en bloc* and without qualification can be most successfully attempted by a refusal to discuss them, or—so far as possible—to allow others to discuss them. That whatever *is* property to-day is rightly so, can only be affirmed by the unscrupulous or by the foolish. All we need require of such a defence is that it should be compelled to begin. Once opened, it provides the replies to its own contentions with automatic efficiency. Private property must be preserved as the guarantee of energy and initiative. Is our proletariat then to be criticized for displaying a deficiency of either; and can we look to that one-eighth of our population which now enjoys to the full the experience of property-holding to supply the community with all it needs of work and enterprise? Property is the just reward of saving. Then how chances it that the easy prodigality of Bond Street does not compel its patrons to change stations with those constrained to a relentless thrift in the Commercial Road? Property is necessary to individual liberty. How then can the Home of Freedom still fail to facilitate its distribution to forty million of her citizens? It is through the operation of private property that society will best be served. Yet in regard to a number of commodities of capital importance a Government Committee assures us that a ring of property holders "are in a position to control output and prices"—and society by means thereof.

The fallacies embodied in such a line of argument do not stand in much need of exposure, they are too glaring to be hid; but they do require to be exactly understood. There *is* a case for the preservation of property, but plutocracy can never urge it; for plutocracy cares nothing for property, save as a means to the establishment of monopoly. It is upon the achievement of some form of monopoly that its most significant energies are concentrated. And whatever the case for extending the opportunities of establishing monopoly rights in private hands and fortifying the position of those who have acquired them, it bears no resemblance to the familiar defence of property. Monopoly, once achieved, offers no prospect of enterprise and initiative: it renders them superfluous. Monopoly is not the reward of saving; it is the result of power, accident, or double-dealing—often of all three. Monopoly does not extend personal liberty: it assists still further to extinguish it. If it operates to serve society, it does so capriciously and precariously; more often it merely exploits the public struggling in its relentless grip, and subjugates the very mind and spirit of men, enforcing upon them its sordid standards and its cruel codes.

II

It is the purpose of this book to make plain that the ideal of Christendom is neither a mediæval Utopia nor merely an inspiring "spiritual myth," but a vital conception of the most immediate and practical significance. It offers the clue, and the only complete one, for want of which society lies in bondage to confusion and despair. And this is true in particular of the problem of property. The Christendom ideal points to that perfect harmony between personal freedom and social function in which property becomes as much an organ of society as it does an expression of personality. For "a society in which the free activities of men are gathered together to create a social order which can be offered as a gift to the glory of God" cannot depend either upon subjective rights of property-holding irresponsibly exercised, nor upon objective functions categorically imposed. Property would exist in such a society to enable man to enjoy that independence which is a condition of his contribution to the common purpose being rightly made: a divine motive would be ever present to reveal that common purpose to every man, so that he would realize more fully than purely mundane considerations will ever enable him to do, that fellowship is life and lack of fellowship is death.

Personal freedom and social function—these are the pillars of the Kingdom of God, and all social institutions must be built round them. To say that we have here the clue to the problem of property is not to say that we are enabled thereby to resolve all its difficulties. We shall have to pick our way patiently through many of them in the course of this chapter, and many more lie outside its scope. But an attempt can be made in the light of the Christendom ideal to establish the contention that on the one hand the opportunities involved in true property-holding are a valid part of the vocation of every citizen who does not choose voluntarily to abjure them; while on the other the preeminent obligations of fraternity must determine the conditions in which those opportunities are exercised. Property, in short, is a part of freedom; but while it must not evaporate into Collectivism, it equally must not degenerate into private monopoly.

We have seen already how this latter degeneration has ended by distorting the very nature of property, as it began by distorting its purpose. The origin of this evil process is not obscure. Property began to be conceived of as having rights unlimited and absolute when, with the break-up of the mediæval order in face of the corruptions of authority, liberty began to be thought of not as an attribute of citizenship, but rather as a right purely individual. Loss of the idea of a social purpose—such as the Christendom ideal so uniquely supplies and illuminates—obscures the social and relative natures of both liberty and property. In the reaction against the results of this error, men tend to conclude that liberty and property are things of which the average person cannot be trusted to make a good use; the State must take charge of them and "ration" them discreetly. Private property allied to unrestricted individualism having issued in private monopoly, the reformer sees no alternative but the establishment of a public monopoly in the economic resources of society. It is a desperate remedy, for it delivers the community into the hands of its politicians and magistrates; and freedom finds new bureaucrat but old capitalist writ large.

But before we turn to consider the validity of the socialist attitude to property as it is ordinarily understood, it is necessary to dispute finally and without any reservation the possibility of any solution for the problem of property being discoverable along the lines of the plutocratic evolution of to-day. For the prime characteristic of modern property rights is that they carry with them power over the lives of others and the destinies of society in general.

The capitalist, in virtue of his industrial power, controls the working condition of thousands of wage-slaves; the financier, by the exercise of a power more subtle but more absolute, determines the very nature of production by his monopoly of credit, and subjugates employer and consumer alike. The concentration of property means the domination of society by the power of money, an influence entirely illegitimate in any true community. Its effect is inevitably disruptive, uneconomic, and capricious. No brotherhood could survive the concession of increased

power and influence to any of its members on the ground
of material possessions, and no society can approximate
to a brotherhood while it still does so. Yet who will be
found to deny that the influence of money-power is the
prime feature of our civilization? The results are glaring and all perceive them: to say that they are anti-social
is a statement of the case not only moderate, but one
which has the further merit of being exactly accurate.
A prodigal recklessness in the opulent few is matched by
a desperate recklessness in the destitute many; while
between them sways an incoherent mass who cling to
"property," so far as they have any experience of it,
with an uninquiring timidity, content that the few should
control the land if they be but allowed to cling to the
rocks of the island of plutocracy. If the moralization
of property is to be begun, we must banish the wretched
contemporary caricature of it from our minds, and redeem the institution from its degradation before a new
tyranny rises up to revenge itself upon the old.

III

Property rights in private hands have become the
means to the exercise of power over those deprived of
them and a stimulus to anti-social greed: let the community extinguish those rights by possessing itself of
them, and these devastating evils will disappear. Such
has been the basic doctrine of the Socialists. Its superficial cogency may be admitted, but its enunciation must
needs be (as it has in fact been), but the prelude to an
exhaustive discussion of the limits of its applicability;
the kinds of property requiring such treatment and susceptible of it; the nature of the social organization to
which it can be safely entrusted; the stages through which

such a development ought to or may require to pass. How little Socialists themselves have agreed about these things is generally known, and every fresh endeavour to explore such problems only accentuates this complexity. But two main schools may be discerned, though the practical differences between them are perhaps fewer than their disciples realize.

To consider first the implications of Communism. The word was for long an essentially academic one; and many an Anarchist-Communist indulged in his dream of the common use at individual discretion of goods and services which it was nobody's particular obligation to provide, without gaining more attention than proposals of so little relevance to circumstances ordinarily received.[1]   A few critics stayed to point out that not only did such a conception involve a degree of enlightened individualism impossible to attain in any community fortuitously composed, but that such an amorphous society could never exhibit the vitality, to say nothing of the efficiency, of one in which the positive value of social institutions which corresponded to essential functions was realized and exemplified.   But the Russian revolution and its international reverberations have swept this version of Communism into oblivion, and recalled to us that the authentic origins of the term must be looked for in a Manifesto of 1847 and an uprising of 1871.   We have said something in an earlier chapter of the Communist experiment to-day, and its relation to our ideal.   In regard to property, it can certainly be said that the Soviet Republic has made a more complete and ruthless attempt

[1] Not every exponent of Anarchist-Communism was so light-heartedly unsystematic as this of course.   Some of the contemporary Guild Socialists would claim Kropotkin as a forerunner of their ideals and even of their proposals.

to entrench upon the rights of private ownership and individual discretion than has ever been made in the history of the world. The attempt has been made and it has failed, and the policy is already in many important respects being abandoned. It has failed because initiative being destroyed, and liberty, individual and corporate, existing only on sufferance, no inducement could arise to replace the sordid motives on which capitalism has relied. Peasants, whose livelihood had depended on the wise development of their property, found themselves harrassed and menaced by a bungling bureaucracy, until they lost all motive to produce for more than their own immediate needs. Industrial workers found themselves as much divorced as before from control over the property on which they worked and still largely subject to an external dictatorship in matters of labour discipline. Communism, in the name of the public interest, has concentrated all the tyrannies of irresponsible private property in itself, destroying the capitalist, and making the financier obsolete, but only by "shifting the credit basis from the bank-note to the machine gun."[1]

Russian Communism has certainly demonstrated that the public absorption of property can render rich men poor, but the more crucial problem of making poor men richer has not been solved thereby, nor will it ever be if by "richer" we mean, as we should, richer in freedom and richer in opportunity as well as in material possessions. The Socialist of the Collectivist type is ready enough to criticize Communist methods, but his programme is not greatly different in aim; though he has often been able to appreciate that the indiscriminate pro-

[1] *Credit-Power and Democracy*, by C. H. Douglas, p. 63. The economic implications of the Bolshevik policy are very well brought out in Chapters V. and VI. of this remarkable book.

vision of communal services at the public expense is
rather a limitation of freedom than an expansion of it,
since ultimately it dictates the nature of the individual's
expenditure, instead of leaving this a matter of personal
choice. Moreover, the Socialist is generally at pains to
make clear that he has no desire to interfere with rights
over private property save in so far as these are a part
of "the means of production, distribution and exchange."
The definition is a wide one, and the questions it raises
are not simple. One question above all is of capital importance, and has never been more engagingly stated
than it was twenty years ago in a characteristic hyperbole by one of the very few critics of Socialism who have
exhibited both a passion for democracy and a sense of
humour.

"I have a number of friends who agree with me in
thinking this, that art should not be competitive or industrial, but most of them go on to the very strange
conclusion that one should not own one's garden, nor
one's beehive, nor one's great, noble house, nor one's
pigsty, nor one's railway shares, nor the very boots on
one's feet. I say, out upon such nonsense! Then they
say to me, what about the concentration of the means of
production? And I say to them, what about the distribution of the ownership of the concentrated means of
production? And they shake their heads sadly, and say
it would never endure; and I say, try it first and see.
Then they fly into a rage."[1]

Before we accept the claim of central authority to
entrench itself, in the name of a formula, upon the
sphere of ownership, let us be clear to ourselves what is
the essence of ownership and of how much is the citizen
deprived who has no experience of it. The true meaning

[1] H. Belloc, *The Path to Rome*, p. 111.

of ownership does not lie in any abuses of power or gain to which it is subject, but in the assurance of security, the sense of responsibility, the opportunity for self-direction, freedom of choice and some form of arranging one's own life in advance. The effect of the absence of such powers the following passage will suggest:

"The vast mass of workers in our towns have long ago ceased to have any right of possession over the tools or materials of their occupation;   .   .   . they have no secure-footing of their own, no self-dependent area on which to fall back, no reserved resources which are under their own control and direction. Their existence is never in their own hands; nor are they responsible for their own maintenance. The stability, the power to look before and after, the assured hold on reality, the embodiment of their wills in a material fact, which we philosophically recognize to be the moral and spiritual value of private ownership—all this is denied to them. They enjoy no sense of background such as would endow their individual lives with a certain dignity. They exist on the surface; they cannot strike roots and establish permanency. . . . It is just the moral discipline of responsible ownership which they are bound to lack."[1]

It is clear that these attributes of liberty and citizenship must be restored to the masses in a free society: it is not clear that a purely public ownership either would or could restore them. Just as State service without guild control cannot afford men freedom in the industrial sphere, so State monopoly without some guaranteed share in the social inheritance for every individual cannot provide them security in the economic one. Not the prohibition of property rights but their moralization is what we

[1] Canon Scott Holland in the volume of essays entitled *Property: its Duties and Rights.*

have to aim at if we are not to put the individual at the mercy of the political authorities. We have to see what light Christian tradition may throw on such a process, and what practical developments it may involve for society to-day.

IV

It will be clear from the standpoint already elaborated in this chapter that the moralization of property cannot be brought about merely by a discreet and benevolent exercise on the part of existing property owners of rights now legally belonging to them, irrespective of the nature of such property or the present distribution of it. The moralization of property-holding involves a new outlook, not merely upon the obligations of it, but upon the sanctions which give it a title to exist. Anything less than this is not only utterly inadequate in principle, but it is very largely ineffective in practice. It has often been urged, for instance, that the claims of the worker to a "full life" must be the first change upon the industry in which he is engaged; and a body of shareholders have even combined in a public statement to declare their conviction "that the claims of the workers to wages making it possible for them to live a full and free life come before the claims of shareholders to dividends"; and that they "are prepared to accept whatever personal loss shall arise" through the reorganization involved to produce such a result. The declaration was by no means without value in some respects, but it could have no practical bearing on the present organization of industry, since that organization is from beginning to end devised to produce money values, and money values only, and would immediately become ineffective if efforts were made to adopt it to humaner purposes without radical change. The purposes of industrial activity to-day are ultimately determined by finance, and while the community allows the functions which finance so inadequately performs to be exercised by private corporations for their own enrichment, the emancipation of industry and the moralization of property will remain equally unrealizable.

Yet another theory, and a very dangerous one, is often advanced among Christians as providing a sufficient justification of property rights in their present form, or something not widely different from it. This is the doctrine of "stewardship." It is contended that great riches, so far from being regarded as the fruit of avarice, the seed of tyranny, and the means of luxury, ought to be looked upon as affording a unique opportunity for the exercise of benevolence and charity. The argument is not generally stated so plainly, but in a confused sort of way it has been employed to add a welcomed sanction to the "deceitfulness of riches." It is necessary to observe that this comfortable theory contains not only a spiritual falsehood, but an economic fallacy, for such a "stewardship" is outside the ability of any individual to execute. The ability to lay out money wisely is, like other human capacities, strictly limited; and luxury expenditure, in which form "benevolence" so often clothes itself, is normally a process so uneconomic as to be anti-social. The administration of wealth is not a "stewardship," it is a dictatorship; since riches involve a power over others, degrading alike to those who are possessed of it and to those who are its passive dependents.[1]

----

[1] I do not wish to be taken as denying the personal responsibility of the individual Christian in regard to the investment and expenditure of the wealth of which he finds himself in charge under our prevailing social arrangements. I seek only to deny that the exercise

It is recorded of a brilliant leader of fashionable society to-day, that on someone remarking in her hearing, "After all, you cannot serve God and Mammon," she interposed with the characteristic comment, *"I can!"* It is a wide-spread, if largely a secret conviction. Men feel that the perils of wealth, however subtle and universal, can somehow be circumvented in their own particular case. It is an impression, however, for which no grounds are to be discovered in the Gospels; and Christ, who "came to fulfil the Law and the Prophets," endorsed in doing so the most resolute and elaborate attempt to achieve the moralization of property that has ever, perhaps, been made by an organized community.[1] Read, as it should be, in the light of the Mosaic code as a whole, the Eighth Commandment, says Dr. Bartlett, "tells against all accumulation of land and wealth as 'private Property' which affects inequitably and oppressively the opportunities and welfare of men and women, as God's own special property." The prophets arose to testify to the apostasy involved in social injustice and to develop and uplift that ideal of the Kingdom which Christ Himself, as the greatest of them, made, as has been already demonstrated,[2] the very essence of His teaching. In the demand that His followers should "seek first the Kingdom of God and His righteousness" so that thereby all other things should be added unto them, He was uttering no recommendation to a mere idle personal piety sustained by the

of that responsibility, however admirably fulfilled, can ever be a sufficient substitute for complete social reorganization, even though every individual Christian strove his utmost to be worthy of his opportunities.

[1] See the essay by Dr. Vernon Bartlett in *Property: its Duties and Rights.*

[2] See above, Chapter IV.

work of others, but a declaration that only in a community of fellowship and justice can men hope to find their material problems solved.

It is not possible within the limits of this chapter, nor is it necessary, to trace the developments through which Christian doctrines as to property rights have passed nor the causes which have influenced them. At two epochs of history, however, does the attitude of the Church seem to have been of crucial importance—the moment when she first found the forces of government no longer in bitter hostility, but offering an official alliance, and the period during which her teaching had its completest influence over the newly-developed civilization of Christian Europe. The first of these two supreme opportunities found the Church spiritually unprepared and morally unequal to her mission of "over-coming the world." For whatever reasons—and it is not difficult to discern them [1]—the Faith had lost that aggressive quality, that power of moral initiative which could alone have built a new and noble civilization out of the crumbling ruins of the Roman world. "The social order remaining at this crucial point unadjusted to the full spirit of the Gospel of Divine Fatherhood and Human Brotherhood, came to react adversely on Christian ideals of property generally. Broadly speaking, the idea of property as a social and economic institution really remained pagan and, so far as embodied in law, Roman in its spirit and presuppositions. . . . Civic and economic life was in principle left to go its own way according to its own secular and selfish laws, as a system outside the redemptive control of Christian motives and methods." [2]

[1] See Dr. Bartlett's above-mentioned essay, pp. 108–116.
[2] *Property: its Duties and Rights*, pp. 113, 115.

V

From this failure to rise to the height of her mission the Church has never wholly recovered. The moment when she will finally realize and fulfil it is still in front of her.

Nevertheless, the attempt made by the mediæval Church to develop a body of teaching which should cover every aspect of man's social life was, for all its defects, a very noble one, and the ideal of Christendom was prefigured, even if it was not exemplified, in it. The theory of property which formed the basis of mediæval economics had been evolved through long centuries of Christian thought upon the subject, and it found its most characteristic and elaborate exposition in the writings of Aquinas. The sanctions for private property-holding according to this theory were essentially social, and Aquinas refused to recognize any private right in property, since a man must hold those things which are his as for the common use and must minister of what he has to the necessities of others. Aquinas found a justification for private property in three considerations, all of which contributed to the common interest: it provided an incentive to energy; it facilitated the better ordering of human affairs by affording to each his particular function in the task of procuring goods for the community; and it provided a basis for social peace and order by giving to each his particular share to look after. Whatever the validity of this particular vindication of private property, it is clear that it can only have any force—or, indeed, any meaning at all—in reference to a social order in which a share in property and its opportunities was a matter of universal experience. And despite much that was inequitable and tyrannical in the

social conditions of the time, such experience was infinitely more universal than it is to-day.

Mediæval economic teaching, moreover, is of great
importance in that it was employed as an end to the
maintenance of human solidarity, and not—as it has
commonly been in modern times—as an apologia for the
destruction of it.   The distinction is fundamental, and
the cause of it not less so.   It has been explained by a
modern authority in the statement that "the application of
ethics to economic transactions was rendered possible by
the existence of one universally recognized code of
morality and the presence of one universally accepted
moral Teacher." [1]   In short, the ideal of the brotherhood
of man followed upon a recognition of the Fatherhood
of God and the authority of Christ.   The Church in the
Middle Ages certainly enforced far more clearly than it
has ever done since the personal responsibility of each
of its members in matters of social righteousness; yet it
did so in relation to a social ideal—the mediæval conception of Christendom—more comprehensive and more
completely adequate than any political theory or economic doctrine has in later ages been able to provide.

Save in the light of this ideal it is impossible to
perceive the real nature and significance of such practical
exemplifications of mediævalism as the guilds.   Indeed,
it is doubtful whether the historical significance of economic theory can be rightly appreciated unless the
further factor of the "corporate mind" expressing itself
in public opinion and the social action following upon
it is taken into account.   It is evident that a society which
visited "forestallers" and "regraters" with humiliat-
ing—and even savage—punishments, and which exercised a rigid corporate control over price-fixing and the

[1] Dr. George O'Brien in *An Essay on Mediæval Economic Teaching*.

whole sphere of industrial production, had very different ideas about the rights of property from those in ascendancy to-day. The guild system, for instance, was based on private ownership, but it allowed of property only within the governing principles of Vocation and Fraternity. Prices—the weapon of the profiteer—could not be fixed at individual discretion, but had to be corporately determined according to the principle of the "Justum Pretium," which operated not merely to protect the consumer in the maintenance of a standard of quality but also to safeguard the worker's standard of life. Property, moreover, did not ordinarily give the individual employer the right to hire workers on his own terms; these latter were generally apprenticed to the guild as a whole; they had a right of appeal to it against their employer; and they had a reasonable hope of rising to the rank of guild-master in their turn. Even in the countryside, where elements of servitude restricted the independence of the peasant, manorial property did not operate to reduce him to the status of a proletarian, and "the ordinary child was still born into a system in which the basis of his work and livelihood was assured to him." Herr Beer says of the peasants of the 1381 rebellion, "They were not atomized, propertyless proletarians, but partners of agrarian co-operative associations, imbued with the traditions of their ancient liberties and with sentiments of communal life. . . they did not formulate any communist programme, for they were not suffering from a system of private property, but from encroachments upon their common rights, and against these encroachments they rebelled." [1]

It is worth noting that mediæval thought esteemed

[1] *History of British Socialism,* vol. i. p. 20.

industry, commerce, and finance in precisely the opposite order to that in which power and influence belong to them to-day. The association of the idea of property with the obligation of personal activity in connection with it, and the exaltation of work as distinguished from commerce, led to that perfection of the objects of work which resulted in the beauty and stability of mediæval craftmanship. The temptations to avarice in the business of trading were clearly recognized, and the social dangers involved in the abuse thereof were also fully appreciated. Speculative trading was universally condemned, and usury *as a means of livelihood* unsparingly denounced.

But here we come upon a point of considerable importance, for not only does it furnish a significant clue to the forces which were to prove too strong for the effort to develop a complete moralization of property at the end of the mediæval age, but it is highly relevant to any similar one which man may make to-day. For it was the development of finance which partly bewildered and partly defeated the mediæval economic teachers in their attempts to preserve a doctrine of social righteousness in a rapidly expanding world-order. Money had so long been regarded as being fundamentally a medium of exchange (as it ought to be), that it was not for a long time perceived that it could also be employed as "capital," and indeed the opportunity for its being so but slowly emerged. It was, however, gradually borne in upon mediæval writers that a distinction might exist between "usury" and a legitimate payment for the hire of money, or rather money-power; and consequently all sorts of efforts to explore paths which might disclose justifiable sanctions for the exaction of interest were

embarked upon.[1]   But the most important justification
of interest was in fact the practical one which lay in the
increasing necessity for credit, while no organization
(save such small and inadequate experiments as the
montes pietatis) for the communal control and issue of
credit-power was in existence. Before this problem fell
not only the mediæval economic theory, but the actual
social achievement of that noble approximation to the
Christendom ideal which the Middle Ages in some directions really attempted.[2] If the origin of the problem
was spiritual in essence, it was none the less one of very
practical implications, and strikingly similar in both
respects to that by which society is so crucially confronted to-day.

VI

It is not within the scope of this chapter to trace the
change of ideas as to the basis of property rights after
the breakup of mediæval society, spiritual and secular.[3]
It has glanced at mediæval conceptions of property only

[1] An interesting and exhaustive account of these is given by Dr.
O'Brien, *op. cit.* chapter iii. section 2.

[2] Space does not permit the discussion of how far the centralization, so largely implicit in mediæval Catholicism, was a factor in
the decline of the society it dominated. In the sphere of economics
it certainly tended to impose a rigidity which, despite the ingenuity
of ecclesiastical writers on the subject, made it impossible for them
to maintain the relation between moral values and social practice in
an age of technical and commercial expansion. The danger of
rigidity is never absent from centralization, whether it be that of
Leninism, of International Finance, or of Papal Autocracy.

[3] See on this subject the chapter by H. G. Wood in *Property: its
Duties and Rights*; also chapters ii. and ix. in R. H. Tawney's *The
Acquisitive Society,* to which book the present writer is greatly in-
debted, particularly in respect of the admirable chapter on "Property
and Creative Work."

because these serve to illuminate both the strength and limitations of the Christendom ideal as it was dimly grasped by the Middle Ages. It is often urged by critics of mediæval society that the men of that time were at least no better individually than are men to-day; that they continually exhibited a failure to live up to their own standards, and that the literature of the age teems with denunciation of avarice and corruption. The truth of these criticisms (which is often exaggerated) does not affect the validity of the contention that in the attempt to formulate and maintain a moral basis for economic activities, mediæval society was showing itself conscious of the fact that such an attempt was an absolutely indispensable prelude to the achievement of any sort of social justice and stability whatsoever. Men organized deliberately to make ideals of Vocation and Fraternity a social reality and to render more difficult the emergence of those evil proclivities which economic operations are always liable to arouse in the human breast. When we regard the achievements of mediæval craftmanship we may feel content to judge the society that produced them by its work. But it is far more important to judge it by its faith. For that Faith, however dimly we perceive its social implications, or fail to apply them to the whole of our life, is the Faith of Christendom; and it is in the light of it that we must go forward to the new social order, by the unfolding of which the Church may yet come once again to the rescue of the world.

We have reached the culmination of plutocracy. "The institution of property has, in its modern form, reached its zenith as a means of giving to the few the power over the life of the many, and its nadir as a means of securing to the many the basis of regular industry,

purposeful occupation, freedom, and self-support."[1]
While this is true, it is still the case, however, that to
many thousands in the "middle classes," a slender hold
on "property" exists, and represents the one social
reality of which they will never willingly let go on any
plea whatsoever.   And this is not from any peculiar
reverence for riches, nor, in the majority of cases, from
any special desire to accumulate them, but simply from
the conviction that only through property comes the
power to make provision for the morrow and resist, if
need be, the dictation of others.   The grounds for such
a tenacity are, then, natural enough; but the effects of
it to-day are disastrous because it is almost entirely
instinctive, and rallies to the defence of the most
monstrous preogatives and monopolies if only the definition of property can somehow be stretched to include
them.   And stretched it accordingly is,[2] so that the most
indispensable personal tools and the most flagrantly unjustifiable tolls are not only defended by the same arguments by the unscrupulous champions of wealth, but
subject to the same criticisms by the enemies of it.   The
humblest annuity-holder thus enrols in the bodyguard
of plutocracy, and every shaft of the Socialist assailant
serves only to confirm him in his unwarrantable
allegiance.

While the forces continue thus aligned the struggle
for emancipation will never succeed, and the money-lord
will be left in the secure supremacy of his golden castle.
Indeed he will only be driven from there when every
valid interest in the community realizes the fatal influ-

---

[1] Professor L. T. Hobhouse in *Property: its Duties and Rights,*
p. 23.

[2] For the widely varying nature of existing property rights, see
The Acquisitive Society, pp. 57, 67.

ence of the dominion exercised by the organized avarice of financial power. It is to this power ultimately, and not to any normal forms of property, that all economic policy is now subservient. It is a power operating behind an effective smoke-screen of technical obscurities and fallacious assumptions. Finance, indeed, is the black magic of our age. Men of all classes offer it obsequious worship even while they groan beneath its sinister effects. They imagine it facilitates the production of what society needs; in fact it is precisely such production that it thwarts. They imagine its pronouncements are beyond dispute; in fact the first condition of all social betterment is that these should be disputed. The task was one in urgent need of being taken up; it has been so, and the unspoken challenge of Finance is now answered.[1] That answer, however, whatever its merits, can only concern us here in so far as it throws light on the nature of some contemporary "property rights" and helps us to distinguish the abuses of money-power from the attributes of a sane conception of ownership.

Without space to elaborate the matter, it must be boldly affirmed that behind the problem of property lies the problem of credit. And the problem of credit requires as a first condition of its solution a general recognition of the source from which it is ultimately derived, and a determination to establish a communal control of it which shall be consistent therewith. For that source is of course the community itself, with that heritage of

[1] The writer is referring to the case presented by Mr. C. H. Douglas in his striking and original books *Economic Democracy* and *Credit-Power and Democracy*. His general agreement with that case is not shared by all the collaborators in this volume, and for the deductions derived from it in the following pages he is alone responsible.

invention, skill, and material resources which by this time gives to it the ability to produce substantially all that its members, as consumers, demand. This ability to produce what is actually required constitutes the *real* credit of the community, yet the issue of credit to facilitate production is not now under any sort of communal control whatsoever. On the contrary, it is in the hands of half-a-dozen banking amalgamations of enormous power, which constitute what is virtually a money-trust on which the whole sphere of industry is dependent. Moreover, the considerations on which the issue of bank credit depend are financial merely; they bear no relation to the needs which a truly social production would be concerned to satisfy, but are concerned only with the probability of the capitalist organizations which apply for credit facilities being able to recover in prices from the public the equivalent of the purchasing power which such an issue of credit represents.

It is no part of our present task to trace all the consequences of this fatal system, though it is of the first importance that their full effects should be generally appreciated. Our purpose in calling attention to the conditions of credit-issue to-day is to emphasize the fact that they give to the controllers of credit the power of actually creating the equivalent of money, and taxing those whose activities require the concession of credit for the use of it. Such a power is the most extreme, as it is the most perilous, example of property rights arising from monopoly which plutocracy affords, the most fundamental usurpation of communal rights which it has achieved. A money-trust controlling credit working in conjunction (and often in actual combination) with industrial trusts controlling prices, and taking from the public not only the cost of the article produced, but the cost of maintaining and improving the means of producing further articles, besides the amount needed to repay the bank for the financial credit conceded, represents an interpretation of property which, communally considered, verges upon insanity. It permanently impoverishes the many to serve only the most sordid interests of the few; it frustrates the production which, scientifically employed, could fully satisfy, with a tithe of existing effort, the reasonable needs of all; and substitutes for that universal claim on the communal inheritance through the exercise of which men could gain security and freedom, the fortification of monopolies by which the masses are rendered needy and enslaved.

VII

How, then, in our conception of a returning Christendom are we to envisage the future of property? Must we regard it as an institution incapable any longer of proving to be of service to society? Is the social control of avarice so impossible that private liberty and individual discretion must be surrendered altogether to State organization and public monopoly? Such a prospect is not inviting. The most relentless thinker, who is at the same time the most thorough-going practical exponent of modern Socialism, has thus depicted it. "Socialism," says Lenin, "is impossible without large capitalist technique constructed according to the last word in science, *without systematic State organization subjecting millions of people to the strict observation of a uniform standard of production and distribution of products.* We Marxians have always said this, and it is hardly worth wasting even two seconds in arguing this point with people who do not understand it." [1]   The implications of the public monopoly of all economic functions could hardly be more plainly stated, and thus stated, we see them to be wholly incompatible with the social values inherent in the Christendom ideal.   On the other hand, we have seen how impossible is the moralization of property without the repudiation of an economic system based primarily upon money values, and a readiness to revise the basis upon which property rights can establish a legitimate claim to social recognition.

This book has not been written to formulate a precise social programme, but to present an ideal and to make clear what is involved in it.   The vision of Christendom reveals men contributing in freedom to the common purpose of building up a social order which can be offered to God as something consonant with His will for mankind which He has created, loved, and enfranchised. What such a large and splendid conception implies in the worship of the Church, in the organization of work and in the realization of human brotherhood other chapters suggest; what is written here of its bearing upon property must be read in conjunction with them, if its place in the whole scheme is to be appreciated.

Its implication in regard to property may perhaps be best suggested by the adoption of a familiar distinction. In property for *use* every citizen must be afforded his personal share: property for *power* as it exists to-day must be transmuted into communal functions, regulated

[1] See his article on "The Meaning of Agricultural Tax" in the *Labour Monthly*, July 1921, p. 21.   The whole article is profoundly significant, as when on p. 23 he observes: "Capitalism is an evil in comparison with Socialism, but Capitalism is a blessing in comparison with Mediævalism."

not by the whim of officials, but according to defined and generally recognized principles. The destruction of private monopoly involves the vesting of credit-issue in communal organizations, while price regulation must depend no longer on purely financial considerations, but upon the true economic reality involved in the relation of goods consumed to goods produced. These vital changes achieved, the evil attributes of property vanish, since society can no longer be exploited by means of it; and it becomes possible to evolve a social order which, without severing the individual from such hold upon property rights as shall guarantee his independence, shall yet safeguard the community from the anti-social activities for which private monopoly gives scope, and preserve the industrial co-operation which, whatever technical developments may emerge in a free society, is likely to be involved in the economic structure of the future.

The latter point is an important one, since the few champions of a distributed property who have arisen in this monopolistic age have tended to neglect the social basis of modern production. The "Distributivist" has been too exclusively an individualist. Moreover, he has been preoccupied almost solely with the peasant, and with the peasant considered less as a partner in an agrarian community than as an isolated proprietor exercising absolute powers over his own fields. This has given to his position an element not perhaps of unreality, but at least of irrevelance to the main problems by which society is now confronted. What is necessary is to relate the claim of the individual to a personal share in the national inheritance to the facts of social production and industrial solidarity.

Paradoxical as it may appear, a clue to the problem

may perhaps be found in a feature of that form of organization which industrial capitalism adopted in order to enlarge its potentialities—the Limited Liability Company, as a result of which the individual *entrepreneur* gave way to the association of shareholders. "The dividend," says Mr. Douglas in a penetrating passage,[1] "is the logical successor to the wage, carrying with it privileges which the wage never had and never can have, whether it be rechristened pay, salary, or any other alias; because the nature of all these is a *dole of purchasing power revocable by authority,* whereas a dividend is a payment, absolute and unconditional, of something due. The first is servitude, however disguised, the second is the primary step to economic emancipation. . . . It may not be superfluous to point out that there is no more inevitable connection between dividends and 'production for profit' than between 'pay' and Socialism."[2] Whatever might be the ultimate means through which the individual would receive his share of communal product, it would seem that a start might be made in the large and better organized industries by the foundation of a Credit Bank in each case, based on the Industrial Union involved, through which all the salaries and wages of those registered as being engaged in this industry would be paid. Such a bank would differ from the profiteering banks of to-day, which "live by making money and putting it into circulation," in that it would issue capital as occasion arose corresponding to the real credit inherent in the ability of its members to produce (in conjunction with the owners of the plant) what the community

[1] It is necessary to state that the conclusion indicated in this quotation is one from which strong dissent is expressed by at least one contributor to this volume.

[2] *Credit-Power and Democracy,* pp. 43-44.

required from the industry in question. It need only be added that by the issue of such fresh capital, the Labour Bank would enable the workers concerned to develop an encroaching economic control over the product and plant of the industry which would logically end in proprietorship—a proprietorship, however, which could not include the power of fixing prices. Individual workers would, as members of the bank, draw from the industry a progressively increasing dividend irrespective of their pay, which would not cease on their retirement.

These proposals are referred to, without any attempt to elaborate them, since they add practicality to what otherwise might appear as vague and unrealizable ideals. It seems clear to the present writer that the development of industrial credit-banks would provide an economic basis for that revival of guild organization of which mention has already been made in these pages, and which is certainly indispensable to the achievement of industrial self-government for the workers of every grade. Such organization, by entrusting the control of production to those actually engaged in it, and by setting them free to labour without regard to the creation of money-values as such, would bring within sight another aspect of the moralization of property, by affording both the opportunity and the motive for the making of things which should be fitting to their purpose and beautiful in themselves. The vast deluge of ugly and meretricious articles poured out by the commercial system of to-day reflects the sordid and transient motives which induce the production of it. Men with the assured status that economic freedom and industrial responsibility will give them will consent to produce only what they would be proud themselves to own.

The moralization of property will restore dignity and joy not to men only, but to all to which they may turn their hand.   In the Christendom whither our Faith beckons us, God's children will glorify Him by their acts no less completely than with their lips.

THE FAILURE OF MARXISM

BY

REV. NILES CARPENTER, M.A., Ph.D.

Instructor and Tutor in Social Ethics, Harvard University

SYNOPSIS

For the Christian Marxism is an alien force: an examination of its principles reveals the reasons for this.

Marxism is generally held to embody three leading ideas: (1) *The law of capitalist accumulation.* (2) *The class war.* (3) *The materialistic conception of history.* To these a fourth is often added— *the dictatorship of the proletariat,* but this is not accepted as a part of Marxism by all its adherents.

These theories outlined. (1) Centres round the *labour value concept* and leads to the demand for *the abolition of the wage-system.* It has two important corollaries: the theory of the *rate of profit* and the doctrine of *increasing misery.* (2) Is held to have been the moving force of all history and to be the means of the future overthrow of capitalism. (3) Leads to the deduction that this overthrow is inevitable once technical progress reaches a certain point.

Before criticism of these doctrines is undertaken the great value of Marx's work has first to be acknowledged. (1) He dealt a death-blow to old-school economics. (2) His theories all contain important elements of truth. (3) He brought to the cause of Labour brilliant abilities, wide scholarship, and great devotion.

The reader must beware of irrelevant considerations in following the criticism of Marxian doctrines. (1) The great gifts and services of Marx do not guarantee the soundness of his economic and ethical theories. (2) Marxian conclusions must not be embraced without understanding and acceptance of their economic basis. (3) The shortcomings of the Christian Church in the social sphere do not affect the duty of Christians to criticize proposals antagonistic to their Faith.

. *The labour value theory* has been rendered untenable by the attempts of Marx to safeguard it. The effect of the three qualifications made by Marx exposed. Fatal effect of the destruction of this theory in undermining the Marxian position. *The theory of the rate of profit* examined. Labour-value has no real existence. The Marxist's "alleged solution administers a death-blow."

History has not verified the Marxian analysis—notably with reference to *the doctrine of increasing misery.* Neo-Marxist interpretations of this doctrine beside the point. *The abolition of the wage-*

system. The system not the one prime cause of the evils of industrialism—despite the spiritual defects which it exhibits. Its obsolescence suggested.

The doctrine of the class war is (i.) inconsistent in statement; (ii.) an inaccurate account of contemporary alignments; (iii.) abhorrent to Christian morality.

(i.) The proletariat is alternately stated to include "all wage-labourers" and "the lowest stratum of society"—definitions mutually exclusive. Marxist's efforts to escape the dilemma are either honest but futile, or effective but vicious—reasons for this explained. (ii.) The class conflict between employer and employed, however bitter, is but one amongst a number. (iii.) The class war can only be made effective by inciting men to envy, revenge, and covetousness. Christians cannot look to God's Kingdom being built with the works of the Devil.

The materialistic conception of history is dangerous to those who embrace it in (i.) inoculating them with a deadening fatalism; (ii.) fixing their attention entirely on destruction. Moreover, the Christian must further object that the doctrine is metaphysically and ethically incompatible with his Faith. Grounds for this objection explained.

The persistence of Marxism, despite its errors and fallacies, due (i.) to the half-truths which it embodies; (ii.) its moral baseness. Marxism was given to the world at a time when the working-classes already held most of the theories it contained: it crystallized them into a tradition which now persists as such. The class-war doctrine, moreover, which is the heart of Marxism, makes a permanent appeal to the lower nature of men whose social conditions subject them to such a temptation. It is for the Christian to show them "a more excellent way."

CHAPTER VIII

THE FAILURE OF MARXISM

SEVENTY-FIVE years ago a new revolutionary creed was proclaimed, as "already acknowledged by all European Powers to be itself a power."[1] In 1847 the statement may have been flamboyant hyperbole, but it is literal truth in 1922. For the new creed was Marxism, and Marxism to-day is a world power.

Marxism rules a great European nation, while every other industrial country has seen its government over-turned, or threatened by disciples of the creed. To the Christian sociologist such a spectacle is of evil omen. For the progress of Marxism betokens to him the advance of an alien force, which must be driven from the territory it now occupies before the work of building a Christian industrial society can be begun. An examination of the principles of Marxism, in the light of economic fact and of Christian ethics reveals the reasons for such an attitude.

It is first, however, necessary to determine what are the leading ideas of Marxism. There is a general agreement that they embody three major theories: *the law of capitalist accumulation,*[2] the *class war,* and *the*

[1] Marx and Engels, *Communist Manifesto.* Introduction.
[2] Marxist terminology is used throughout this discussion, excepting where it is too highly technical for a general treatment of this sort. The reader who finds it difficult may familiarize himself with it by turning to the *Communist Manifesto* and the English translation of *Das Kapital.*

materialistic conception of history.[1] A fourth feature,
the dictatorship of the proletariat, is generally considered a Marxian doctrine, although many Marxists of the
better sort—humanly speaking—repudiate it.

It is possible here to give only the briefest outline of
these theories. The law of capitalist accumulation
centres round the labour value concept, which holds
that "the magnitude of the value of any article" is
determined by "the amount of labour socially necessary
for its production, under normal conditions of production and with the average degree of skill and intensity
prevalent at the time."[2] The unit by which labour is
measured is "simple abstract human labour," to which
various degrees of skilled labour are reduced by a
"social process that goes on behind the backs of the
producers and consequently appears to be fixed by custom." Value, in the sense here used, is *exchange* value;
use value being assumed throughout the Marxian value
analysis. The theory goes on to state that the value of
labour as a commodity—that is, wages—also equals the
amount of labour necessary for its production, to wit,
the duration of labour necessary to produce the food,
clothing, shelter, and the like, necessary to support the
worker and his offspring, but that the number of hours'
labour necessary to compensate the employer for the
worker's wages are less than the number of hours actu-

[1] Beer's rendering of the German *Geschichtsauffassung* is pre-
ferred here to the more common translation "interpretation of
history." Beer, *History of British Socialism,* vol. ii. p. 202.

[2] Marx, *Das Kapital,* vol. i. part 1, chap. i. pp. 6–12, and vol. i.
part 3, chap. vii. sec. 2, pp. 166-180. Quotations and page references are from the Swann, Sonnenschein English translation for
vol. i, from the Kerr American translation for vol. iii.

ally worked; so that the capitalist-employer absorbs the surplus value created by this extra, unpaid-for labour. Rent, interest, and profit are all regarded merely as different forms assumed by the surplus value squeezed out of wage-labour in this way. Indeed, capital itself is held to be accumulated mainly from the same source.[1]

The Marxist concludes from this theory of capitalist accumulation that the root source of existing social injustices is the economic exploitation of the worker through the wage-system. Accordingly, he advocates, as the basic and imperative remedy for these injustices, *the abolition of the wage system.*

Among several important corollaries of this theory two are of particular importance. They are the theories of *the rate of profit* and of *increasing misery.*

The theory of the rate of profit is related to the concept of surplus value. It follows from that theory that the rate of surplus value yielded on any enterprise, relative to the total capital invested in it, varies directly as the proportion of that capital which is spent on wages. That is, since surplus-value is believed to be returned only through exploited wage-labour, the larger the portion of any investment which is put into wages, the higher the rate of surplus-value secured from that investment. Yet the *rate of profit,* by which Marx means the rate of return actually secured on capital in the business world, does not vary in this way. In fact, due allowance being made for risk, luck, monopoly, and the like, the rate of return varies little on different investments. The "bourgeoisie" economist calls this practically uniform yield "pure interest." The Marxist calls it the rate of profit. The Marxist now has to explain the dis-

[1] Marx, *Misère de la Philosophe,* chapter i, section 2, Kerr translation, p. 55. *Das Kapital, loc. cit.*

crepancy between the rate of surplus-value, which, according to his previous analysis, should vary according to the constitution of the capital in each investment, and the rate of profit, which, as he himself perceives, varies hardly at all. The explanation offered by Marx is that competition among capitalists forces the rate of profit actually received by them to a uniform level, equal to the *average* of the surplus-values extracted from their various enterprises. Marx goes on to say that the prices of goods are adjusted so as to make this uniform profit possible, the price in any article being higher or lower than the labour-value embodied in it, according as competition adds to or substracts from the surplus-value accruing from the article. The theory states, further, that the only case in which labour-value and surplus-value really appear is in the total value of all the goods produced in a given competitive area.[1]

The theory of increasing misery can best be set forth in the words of Marx's famous summary: "Along with the constantly diminishing number of the magnates of capital, who usurp and monopolize all advantages of this process of transformation, grows the mass of oppression, slavery, degradation." The downfall of capitalism is to result from this progressive impoverishment of labour. "The monopoly of capital becomes a fetter upon the mode of production itself.—This integument is burst asunder. The knell of capitalist private property sounds. The expropriators are expropriated."[2]

[1] An admirable brief statement of this portion of Marxism is in Beer, *op. cit.* p. 210. Cf. also Marx, *op. cit.* vol. i. part iii. chap. ix. sec. 2, pp. 197–201; chap. xi. pp. 289–294, vol. iii. parts i. and ii.; especially chap. ix. pp. 182-203.

[2] Marx, *op. cit.* vol. i. part iii. chap. xxxii. pp. 788-789. Cf. also Marx and Engels, *op. cit.*, close of sec. 1: "The modern labourer, instead of rising with the progress of industry, sinks deeper and

The second chief feature of Marxism is the class-war. The Marxist declares that the capitalist class, which lives and moves and has its being by robbing the working-class, is in deadly conflict with it, and that the struggle between exploiter and exploited, or bourgeoisie and proletariat, has been so bitter and continuous as to have been the moving force of all history since the industrial revolution. And, as has already been seen, the Marxist expects the class-war to overthrow capitalism, after the proletariat has been goaded to desperation by its increasing misery.[1]

The class-war finds its philosophical setting in the materialistic conception of history, as its economic foundation is furnished by the law of capitalist accumulation. According to the materialistic conception of history, "the mode of production in material life determines the general character of the social, political, and spiritual development of life." From this it is concluded that all changes in the "legal, political, religious, æsthetic, or philosophical ideas of men are merely ideological forms" of the impression made on their minds by the struggles attending transformations in the "economic foundations" of life.[2] The inevitability of the overthrow of capitalist production, once technical progress reaches a certain point, is one of the important deductions of this theory.

deeper below the conditions of existence of his own class. He becomes a pauper, and pauperism develops more rapidly than population and wealth."

[1] The Communist Manifesto is, of course, the very embodiment of the class-war. Cf. also De Leon's "Preamble" to the original I. W. W. "Platform."

[2] Marx, *Zur Kritik der Politischen Oekonomie*, Preface. Cf. also Marx and Engels, *op. cit. sec.* 2, and Marx, *Das Kapital*, Preface to second edition.

The doctrine of the dictatorship of the proletariat is in reality an element of the class-war theory. No separate discussion of it is, therefore, necessary, especially as it is taken up elsewhere.[1] Whatever is said hereafter regarding the class-war may be taken as having force also with reference to the theory of the proletarian dictatorship. It should be noted that this further examination will refer primarily to the class-war and only incidentally to the other; so that those readers who refuse to count the dictatorship of the proletariat as a Marxian doctrine, will find this examination germane to their construction of the theory.[2] The criticism of the doctrine just sketched may now be undertaken.

It should be said, first of all, that much of the work of Karl Marx is of permanent and priceless value to the advancement of social righteousness. He rendered at least three great services. First, he dealt a death-blow to old-school economics. He "showed up" the callousness with which at least some of its ἐπίγονοι regarded labour, and he demonstrated, partly in his own despite, many of their fallacies. Karl Marx jolted political economy out of its bland optimism, and, largely as a result, the political economists are now devoting—as they should

[1] See above, chap. i, sec. 5.
[2] The case against the inclusion of the doctrine in Marxism may be found in Kautsky, *The Dictatorship of the Proletariat*, and Mueller, *Karl Marx und die Gewerkschaften*. For a collection of quotations tending to the opposite viewpoint, cf. Beer, *Karl Marx sein Leben und sein Lehren*, pp. 77–78, and Simkhovitch, *Die Krisis der Social-democratie*, in Conrad's *Jahrbuecher*, vol. vii. 1899. Cf. also Marx and Engels, *op. cit.* sec. 2; and Postgate, *The Bolshevik Theory*, pp. 83-85. Marx used the phrase "revolutionary dictatorship of the proletariat" in his letter criticising the Gotha programme (*Kritik des Gothaer Programs*).

—an increasing amount of thought to the human factor in economic relationships. Again, Marx formulated theories of profound importance, even though not of the degree and kind of significance which he himself assigned to them. In the criticism that follows, attention will be called to the fallacies inherent in such Marxian doctrines as the class-war, the increasing misery of the working-classes, the exploitation theory of wages, and the materialistic conception of history. Yet, for all the inaccuracies involved in their statement, there is an important element of truth in each of them. Marx's insight in perceiving these tendencies is to be acknowledged even though his distortion and over-emphasis of them must be pointed out. Finally, and most important of all, Marx brought to the cause to which he gave his life, immense learning, a brilliant mind, and devoted assiduity. Marx was the first, and probably the greatest, of a line of men who have given the labour movement historical perspective, scientific data, and trained thinking—all of them invaluable. There is an element of tragedy in the fact that most of the "orthodox" Marxists have become so dogmatically attached to the tenets of Marx as to have refused to emulate what is probably his greatest contribution: the application of scholarly method and careful thinking to the problems of industrialism; while one who has possibly, more than any other single man, been true to this, the most valuable feature of Marx's work, has been branded as a "traitor" by the sectaries of the Marxian formulas.[1]

Before criticism of Marxian doctrines can proceed, moreover, the reader is asked not to allow himself to

[1] The reference is to Eduard Bernstein. It is not without significance that one of the most sympathetic appreciations of Marx yet written appears in Bernstein's *My Years in Exile*.

be so swayed by certain considerations, essentially irrelevant, as not to give adequate attention to the main course of the discussion. There are three particular points at which the reader may be sent off at a tangent from the central line of argument, and from which he should be warned.

The first has to do with the attitude of the essay towards Karl Marx. Many persons, who hold—and rightly—that Karl Marx is entitled to respect not to say reverence, become so highly offended at any attack upon his economic and philosophical system—particularly one couched in as vigorous terms as is this one—as to make them almost incapable of reading, let alone of passing judgment upon it. To such a reader it should be said that there is no intention here of casting mud at the tomb of Karl Marx. He was a noble world-patriot and a brilliant thinker. His leadership was invaluable at a time when the European labour movement sadly needed the courage, devotion, and intellect he freely gave to it. *Yet all of these considerations have nothing to do with the final soundness of his economic and ethical theories.* They must be examined, accepted, or rejected on their own merits; they must shine by their own lustre, not by the reflection from their author's halo. Marxism must be studied irrespective of the virtues of its founder. Otherwise it becomes not an intellectual system but a sectarian dogma. John Calvin may have been a hero and a saint, but there is nothing sacrosanct about Calvinism.

A second sort of objection to the criticism which follows may be taken by the reader who can be called the "non-economic Marxist." He has accepted the economics of Marx largely on faith. The main conclusions of Marxism seem to him plausible and relatively simple;

they may be assimilated and acted upon with little reference to the abstract theorizing which he finds difficult and distasteful. He prefers, instead, to build from it to whatever particular proposal he has to make. William Morris seems to have been of this type. To such a man the economic discussion that follows will be deadly dull and irritating. Accordingly, he may impatiently thrust this analysis aside as not worth the trouble necessary to its understanding, and continue contentedly adhering to an economic creed which offers the supreme advantage of being easily comprehended. To him it must be said that error has always been easier to grasp than sound doctrine, and that the road to understanding is always a difficult one. Marxism is specially plausible and inaccurately simple. As will be shown later, its false simplicity is one of its cardinal faults. And the reader cannot, in justice to his own intellectual integrity, consent to give Marxism his allegiance simply because he will not take the trouble to examine systematically either its basic assumptions or its logical implications. It should be added that he may discover, after all, that the ideas which he now bases upon Marxism may not necessarily have to be founded on that dogma at all. Here again reference may be made to William Morris. His theories maintain their vitality entirely irrespective of their supposed relationship to Marxian economics; in fact, the book in which he collaborated with Mr. Bax to attempt the establishment of such a relationship is probably the least read of all his works.

A third type of reader will take violent offence at the other main element of criticism contained in this essay —namely, the attack on Marxism from the viewpoint of Christian ethics. He will, with entire justice, maintain that the Christian Church has all too long acquiesced in a society that has produced the class hatred to which this essay takes objection. The Church has smugly ignored, or pusillanimously abetted the stupid and wicked repression of human personality that has characterized modern industrial life. She has failed to bear witness to the meaning of her gospel for millions of sweated toilers. Such a person feels, therefore, that the Church has lost her right to criticize the unchristian nature of the philosophy of hate which inspires Marxism, inasmuch as she has failed to protest against the conditions out of which that hate has grown. His position is untenable. It amounts to demanding of the Church that she fail to bear witness to her message in the future, because she has failed to do so in the past. The Christian Gospel of righteousness is eternally valid, and the Christian sociologist must be true to that Gospel, even though he may be wearing sack-cloth and ashes for the disloyalty to it of the Church to which he owes allegiance. Fully acknowledging the sinfulness of the conditions out of which class antagonisms have arisen, he must still assert the sinfulness of an intellectual system—even though it is propounded on behalf of the oppressed classes—which perpetuates and embitters such antagonisms.

The law of capitalist accumulation supplies the economic foundation for Marxism, and a very poor foundation it is. It rests upon the labour value theory already outlined. And this theory has suffered the strange fate of having been rendered entirely untenable by the attempts of Marx to safeguard it. Marx was too good a thinker not to see that a crude, unqualified labour theory of value could not hold together. The concept is consequently modified in three respects: first, by admitting the presence of use-value, or, in current terms, utility, in articles of value; second, by allowing only "socially necessary labour" to be used as a source and measure of value; third, by reducing various degrees of skill to "simple" labour, through a "social process."[1]

The first qualification is damaging to the theory; the next two are destructive of it. If it is once granted that use-value must be present in an article, but is nevertheless maintained that duration of labour is the real indicator of value, then the "utility" theorist can equally well admit that labour may have to be present in such an article but maintain that use-value is the real source and measure of value. Furthermore, once it is admitted that other qualities embodied in an article besides the labour involved in its manufacture are necessary to its value, then the labour-value theorem breaks down; for unless such a theory can hold that duration of labour provides the *sole* and *only* determinant of value, it is not a theory of value at all, but simply a one-sided statement of the fact that certain constituents, including labour, enter into the fixing of value.

The stipulations as to "socially necessary labour" and the equation of different degrees of skill by a "social process" provide the final *coup de main* for the theory. They both have the same import. The first is made to meet the obvious objection that, if only duration of labour fixes value, then the longer it takes to make an article the more valuable it will be; so that the enterprising manufacturer will hire all the lazy, crippled, and awkward working-men in the country, in order to capitalize

[1]The writer makes no claim to any originality in the criticisms of Marxist economics here advanced. They were most of them made a generation ago. The recrudescence of unmodified Marxian economics at the present time, however, makes it plain that these criticisms want repeating.

their ineptitude into huge sums of surplus-value. The reply that only "socially necessary" labour, "average degrees of skill," and the like are counted into value, raises the further question as to where and how these are fixed. The answer is plain: they are fixed in the market, where the pull of economic forces, in the process of fixing values of all sorts, also adjusts the relative estimation of different degrees of skill, industry, and the like. That is to say, the labour used by Marx to measure value is that labour whose value has already been fixed.

A clearer case of circular reasoning occurs in the next modification of the theory. Here Marx is confronted with the necessity of determining which among countless gradations of skill in labour shall be used as a unit for measuring labour—how, that is, the labour of the Amsterdam diamond cutter can be compared with the labour of the South African "black boy," who mines the diamonds. Marx's answer that they are all equated in terms of "simple" labour by a "social process" is simply a roundabout way of saying they are given different valuations in the market. The "social process" does not "go on behind the backs of the producers"; it is part and parcel of their economic activities. A man must be an orthodox Marxist before the activities fixing market values can go on behind his back! The statement comes to this: the unit of "simple labour" by which value is measured is the result of the scale of values fixed in the market; exchange-value is measured in terms of a unit that is itself measured in terms of the exchange-values set in the market: *exchange-value is measured in terms of exchange-value.* The circle is complete.

The labour theory of value having been killed, the entire theoretical structure of Marxism dies with it.

No labour-value, no surplus-value; no surplus-value, no exploitation; no exploitation, no class-war;—in short, no Marxism.

The foregoing criticism of Marxism economics has been so compressed that it may not seem entirely conclusive. Those who are still convinced that "there must be something in it" may get further light by considering the theory of the rate of profit. The reasoning by which Marx attempts in this instance to square his theory of surplus-value with the facts amounts to a denial of the validity of the entire Marxian analysis.

It will be borne in mind that value, according to the Marxian definition, is *exchange-value*. Now, unless exchange-value means the actual relation in which goods are bought and sold for one another, allowing for minor fluctuations, it means nothing, and any attempt to discuss value, in the Marxian sense, without giving it such a meaning is tantamount to a giving up of the theory. Yet this is precisely what Marx does in his attempt to account for the uniform rate of profit. He solves the contradiction between this rate, and the variable rate of surplus-value demanded by this theory of labour-value by boldly declaring that labour-value has no part in the prices of goods, that is, in their actual exchange relations. Nor are the prices to which he refers abnormal, momentary fluctuations from a normal exchange relation. They *are* the normal exchange ratio, for they are bound up with the uniform profit. Thus, according to Marx, labour-value, which is the exchange relation of goods, has no place in the normal and actual exchange of goods; that is, labour-value has no real existence.

"Aha!" the Marxist may exclaim, "you forget that the theory expressly states that labour-value and surplus-value *do* have tangible existence. They appear in the

total value of all the goods in any market and from them
are derived the average rate of profit, upon which, accordingly, their market prices depend. The labour theory
of value has not been given up; it has been merely elaborated to fit the complexities of modern economic organization." Just so. But in so far as the explanation is true,
it means nothing; and in so far as it means anything,
it is mere unsupported statement. It is perfectly true
that the value in exchange of all the goods in a market
equals the sum of their respective prices, but this tells
us nothing about the source or distribution of the separate values. The fact that the age of two men together
equals seventy-five years tells us just nothing about the
age of either.

If this statement is to be of any account as an explanation of value, it must mean that the sum total of values
in the market equals the sum total of labour-time represented by the goods in the market. And here the theory
comes right back to its original position of taking one
of a number of constituent elements in the value of goods
and saying that it is the sole source of value—with this
added difference, that the original statement of the
theory attempted to adduce verification from economic
experience, whereas this proposition is expressly cut off
from any reference to actualities, is in fact a sheer speculation. It might just as reasonably assert that the value
of all the goods in the market equals their total radio-
activity, or their total cubical content. If the explanation of the rate of profit is a recantation of all that
precedes it, the attempt to justify the explanation is
simply so much solemn nonsense. "Thus, far from
effecting the solution of the threatened doctrine, this
alleged solution administers a death-blow, and implies

the categorical negation of what it proposes to support."[1]

The Marxist may still return to the attack. "I don't care a tin whistle for your economic theorizing. What I depend upon is reality. Many a great truth has been put in logically defective form, but the truth has withstood its imperfect statement. As a description of capitalist production, Marx's is unimpeachable. History has proven his analysis to be the right one." Very well, let history speak.

If the predictions of Marxism have been fulfilled, then it still deserves respect. Yet it is so abundantly clear that history has *not* borne out Marx's prophecies that the more honest Marxists have been forced to revise their theories, until one doubts whether they can be called Marxists at all. There is no intention to repeat here the detailed statistical and historical data which the "revisionists" have compiled to prove the non-fulfilment of Marxian forecasts.[2] One of the predictions may, however, be briefly examined in the light of historical fact. The theory of increasing misery is one of the most striking and important of them. Not only is the ultimate *débâcle* of capitalism contingent upon it, but it epitomizes the entire Marxist law of capitalist accumulation. Yet if any fact of recent social history is well established, it is that the wage-earner, far from sinking "deeper and deeper below the conditions of existence of his own class," has maintained his position, and, in addition, made a very considerable advance. Statistics

[1] Loria, *Karl Marx,* Allen and Unwin translation, p. 78. Loria, be it noted, is a sufficiently devoted follower of Marx to have been brought out in English by Eden and Cedar Paul.

[2] Especially Bernstein, *Evolutionary Socialism;* Simkhovitch, *Marxism versus Socialism.*

of real and money wages, of pauperism, of tax returns, studies of family budgets—every scientific device for gauging the economic status of the working-class tells the same story. The working-man is *not* worse off than he was in 1860; he is a great deal better off. There has been a set-back for some sections of the population since 1914, but even the most enthusiastic pessimist will not seriously maintain that any appreciable portion has been reduced to the conditions which were general in 1860.[1] Neither has the concentration of the ownership of wealth proceeded according to plan. On the contrary, thanks to the development of savings banks and the investment market, the ownership of industrial capital is more widely diffused than ever before.

Here the Marxist retorts, "Yes, but the *relative* difference between rich and poor is greater than it was; the working-class is proportionately worse off than before, if not actually poorer. As for concentration of capital, it is *control* that counts, and dare you say that, through trusts and banking cliques, control of industry is not becoming more centralized every day?"[2] Possibly; it is a matter of complete indifference to this discussion. Marx had nothing to say about the *relative,* but the *actual* condition of the proletariat. It was to sink "below the conditions of existence"; capitalism was specifically charged with being unable to maintain its own labour force.[3] And capital was to be "monopolized," definitely,

[1] The presence of famine in portions of Europe has nothing to do with the case. The misery which Marx predicted was not to come about by war—capitalist or otherwise, but was to accompany the normal, peaceful progress of capitalist production.

[2] Thus Loria, *op. cit.* pp. 67-69; Postgate, *op. cit.* pp. 30-33.

[3] "It is unfit to rule because it is incompetent to assure an existence to its slave within his slavery." Marx and Engels, *op. cit.* close of sec. 2. If the statement had read "unable to assure a *proper* existence . . . ," it would, of course, be unobjectionable to-day. It is

physically owned by a few "magnates," not merely manipulated by them.[1] Any other prediction was meaningless either as a deduction from the law of capitalist accumulation, or as a precedent condition to the proletarian revolution. The upsetting of the prediction cannot be explained away by substituting for it one which Marx did not and could not logically make. The prophecy has failed, and its failure gives the lie, finally and conclusively, to the economic theories of Marxism.

Let it be kept in mind that there is no idea here to hold a brief for the present industrial structure. It has its faults in plenty, else this book had not been written. Nor is there any intention of conveying the impression that labour is well off, or even is as well off as before 1914, but merely that it is better off than in 1860. Neither is there any desire to credit the blind workings of the system with the advances that labour has made. Trade-union and Government action have undoubtedly played a part of major importance—although Marx denied to trade-unions any lasting value in advancing the worker's status. Finally, as has just been said, there is no idea of ignoring the fact that the *control* of industry is becoming ever more restricted, partly through the machinery of interlocking directorates, holding companies, trade associations, and other familiar phenomena of corporation finance; partly through the growing industrial hegemony of the banker. All this may be true. *But is has*

not to be denied that the worker's standard of life is lower than it should be or might be, but Marx is talking not in terms of a proper standard of life, but of physical existence.

[1] This is not to say that the public control, or even dissolution of monopolies and financial oligarchies, is not of primary importance. It must be insisted, however, that centralized control of a few key industries was *not* what Marx predicted. He thought that all ownership of all productive instruments would pass into a few hands.

nothing to do with the truth or falsity of Marxian economics. It is not enough to say that developments have been "something like" what Marx predicted, any more than it would be proper to praise a doctor for diagnosing a benignant tumour as a cancer. One is "something like the other," but the difference is that between life and death. And there is a life and death difference between Marx's predictions and the facts of industrial development, at least, so far as his own theory is concerned. For it is necessary to the validating of his theory that his predictions should come true *literally and completely.* Only if so carried out are they of value as verifications of his economic theories. Those theories led Marx to the clear-cut conclusion that the worker by hand and by brain would become progressively poorer while the capitalists were seizing more and more of the world's wealth and themselves growing fewer and fewer in number. Unless this has happened—just this, and not "something like it"—his economic theories are belied by the facts.

Finally, it must be remembered that the inquiry into the truth or falsity of Marx's prediction has not been undertaken on its own account, but because of its relation to the general question of the economic basis for the Marxian revolutionary theory. This theory demands the overthrow of the wage-system, as the inevitable and solely sufficient objective of the revolution. It does so because it concludes—in the picturesque language of a great American Marxist—that "the worker is skinned at the point of production out of all but his bare necessities." If this is true—if it is an indubitable scientific fact that every wage-payment necessarily involves the "skinning" of the worker, then the thing to do is to smash the present economic structure, and the wage-system with it. But is is *not* a fact that the payment of wages inevitably involves the yielding of surplus-value to the employer; and the economic ills of the present industrial order can *not* be infallibly cured by the simple process of destroying the wage-system.

Let it be repeated, there are plenty of things the matter with the wage-system, or more precisely, perhaps, with the wage-relation. As the National Guildsmen have made abundantly clear, it involves a debased status, a non-participation in control, and a soul-destroying passivity incompatible with the Gospel of Him who came that humanity might have life, and have it more abundantly. Further, it is possible as Messrs. Douglas and Orage have concluded, that wages, like any form of wealth distribution based on specific productivity, have been rendered obsolete by the complexities of modern industry, and by the growing preponderance of non-human forms of energy. But the demand for the drastic alteration, or possibly the abolition, of the wage-system on grounds such as these is a totally different matter from the Marxian proposal for its supersession. The one sees in the wage-system a symptom of deep-lying economic, psychological, and spiritual disorders, and seeks the modification of that system as an incident in more far-reaching re-adjustments. The other, that is the Marxian proposal, fixes on the wage-system as the *one prime* cause of the evils of industrialism, and its overthrow as the one thing needful for their remedy.[1]

Once the law of capitalist accumulation is shown to be untenable, the scientific basis for class-war also ceases to exist. Yet the doctrine is held by many, irrespective of its economic foundation, if not in spite of it.

[1] It may be further pointed out that the Douglas-Orage denial of the theory of specific productivity carries with it a categorical negation of the Marxian theorem. Cf. Douglas and Orage, *Credit-Power and Democracy*, London, 1920, chapter i.

The Marxist who holds such a position deserves a special word. His position is an impossible one, for he accepts the conclusions based upon premises which he rejects. He thereby lays himself open to the criticism of being either hopelessly muddle-headed, or of being willing to advocate a set of doctrines whose truth he only half believes, but which he continues to preach because of their propaganda value. And there is evidence that the more thoughtful Marxists are beginning to realize their plight.

Yet the Marxists may indignantly deny being either muddled or disingenuous.[1] He may stoutly declare, "I don't care a snap of the fingers whether my belief in the class-war is based on good economics or not. It is a fact, a horrid, ugly fact. And those of us who have any regard for the common man had better leave off prating about theories and jump in to help him loose once-for-all the capitalist's death-grip on his throat. After all, the class-war is the heart and soul of Marxism." In this last statement, at least, he is entirely correct. Marxism is, primarily, a systematic *apologia* for the class-war. But what of the class-war?

The doctrine is, in the first place, inconsistent in statement; it is, further, an inaccurate account of contemporary class alignments; and, finally, it is abhorrent to Christian morality.

The formal difficulty relates to the nature of the parties involved in the class-conflict. The capitalist, or bourgeois class is fairly obvious so far as Marxism

[1] Eden and Cedar Paul, Foreword to Allen and Unwin translation of Loria, *Karl Marx*, p. 28. Beer, *Karl Marx, sein Leben und sein Lehren*, pp. 111-113. Herr Beer displays praiseworthy frankness. After declaring that the theories of value and surplus-value are the "battle-cry of the proletariat against the bourgeoisie," he calls them "theoretical fiction."

goes. It is "the class of modern Capitalists, owners of
the means of social production and employers of wage
labour." The proletariat is not, however, so easily
identified.

The *Communist Manifesto*[1] formally defines it as "the
class of modern wage-labourers who, having no means of
production of their own, are reduced to selling their
labour power in order to live." But, later on it describes
the proletarian as: "without property; his relation to his
wife and children has no longer anything in common
with the bourgeoisie family relation; modern industrial
labour has stripped him of every trace of national character. Law, morality, religion are to him so many bourgeois prejudices."[2]   In other words, the proletariat,
according to this account, does not include "all wage-
labourers," but only those whom the same document calls
later "the lowest stratum of society." Now, the proletariat cannot be two things at once. It cannot contain
all those who sell their labour-power—skilled, unskilled,
managerial, clerical, and manual—and at the same time
be so poverty-stricken as to be beneath hope of family
life and morality and religion—bourgeois or otherwise.

The difficulty can be explained, but not solved. The
first definition fits into the Marxian economic theories;
while the second accords with the facts. If only the
economic theory would "work out" as the doctrine of
increasing misery predicts that it should, there would be
no contradiction, for all of those who sell their labour-
power would have sunk, long since, into the wretched
resourcelessness envisaged by the second definition. But,
unfortunately for the theory, large numbers of wage and
salary earners perversely refuse to be dragged into the

[1] Marx and Engels, *op. cit.* section 1 (footnote).
[2] Marx and Engels, *op. cit.* close of section 1.

depths of misery, and even receive recruits from the depths below. The class-war theory is inconsistent, because stubborn fact refuses to conform to Marx's dark-hued prophecies as to the future of the working-classes.

The Marxists can meet the dilemma in either of two ways. The first is honest but futile: the second is more or less effective but vicious. The first measure is to tell the better-paid worker that he ought to feel as badly off as his brother in the slums, that he really is a poor, down-trodden wage-slave, and that he should at once cast in his lot with his humbler brother. Such exhortations must always fail miserably. Whatever hope there may be of bringing the residents of St. John's Wood and Poplar together on the basis of their common faith or their common citizenship, they will never be united on the basis of their common economic status, because it does not exist.

On the other hand, the Marxist of the more practical sort perceives the hopelessness of any real organizing of the "salariat" for the purpose of the class-war, and more or less deliberately turns his attention to the proletariat of "the lowest stratum." That is, he respects Marx the propagandist, more than Marx the theorist, and seeks to recruit for the class-war the wretched and the hungry and the hopeless. It is the kind of tactics popular among those Marxists who pride themselves upon being "realists" and genuine dyed-in-the-wool "revolutionaries." And if revolution consists in kicking up a really terrible rumpus, it is very good tactics. Indeed, results—of a sort—generally have been obtained, since the days of Tiberius Gracchus, from an invitation to the poor for the dispossession of the rich. In fact, it will be shown later that just because the Marxian class-war doctrine makes such an appeal, it gains much of its vitality. Nevertheless, such a class-war, inevitably carried on by a fraction of those who sell their labour-power, cannot by any stretch of the imagination claim to be "the movement of the immense majority in the interests of the immense majority." When the leaders of a class-war of such dimensions attempt to justify its excesses and anomalies by pleading the "interests of the immense majority," they are talking nonsense. A class-war of this sort is carried on in the interests of a minority, irrespective of the interests of the majority, and often in opposition to them.

To all of this the "revolutionary" Marxist will probably remain impervious. "I am not concerned with consistencies or inconsistencies," he says, "and am not at all worried if the proletariat is not so all-inclusive as Marx predicted. It is sufficiently large to make plenty of trouble for the capitalist class. Furthermore, in the sense that the struggle between employer and employed is an expression of the class-war, it is the biggest social fact in contemporary civilization. The one great social cleavage to-day is that of labour versus capital." The only trouble with this statement is that it isn't so.

There is no need to preach "industrial pacifism" to establish this point. There is plenty of antagonism between employer and employed. Generally speaking, their relations are those of armed truce, frequently broken by bitter and devastating war. But there are *other* class-conflicts.[1] Here in the United States, we can distinguish at least three others, one of which leads to frequent disorder and death: white versus black, native

[1] A class is taken here as meaning "a number or body of persons with common characteristics, or in like circumstances, or with a common purpose." *New Standard Dictionary.*

versus immigrant,[1] city versus country.[2]   There is not
one class-war, but several, all going on at once, each
ignoring and occasionally overriding the others.   At
times the struggle between capital and labour dominates;
at times other conflicts force it into the background,[3] and
it is mere verbal jugglery to call the other struggle a
"phase" of the capital-labour conflict, because the capitalist takes advantage of it.   As well say that a wind
taken advantage of for a gas attack, during the late
War, was a "phase" of the War!

The class-war doctrine fails to square with the facts
both with respect to the alleged identity of the proletariat
with the wage and salary-earning class, and with respect
to its attempt at the resolution of all class conflicts into
that between capital and labour.

Yet the Marxist can probably not be budged by considerations of this sort from a dogma of such matchless
propaganda value as the class-war.   But the propaganda
it spreads is the sort which constitutes a negation of
Christian morality.   It rests upon motives incompatible
with the Christian ideal.   In so far as the theory has any

[1] The persecution of "Bolsheviks" in America during the winter
1919-1920 was largely an expression of a long-accumulated hostility
towards "foreigners."   The recently-enacted restriction immigration
law indicates the lengths to which this feeling has gone.

[2] The rurally elected legislature of the State of Connecticut has
sought to recall the charter of the city of Hartford, because of the
latter's refusal to abide by an anti-daylight-saving law, passed in
the interests of the farmers.   Hostility between New York city and
"up-state" legislators in New York state politics is proverbial. Great
bitterness has been aroused by the recently organized Congressional
"farmers' bloc."

[3] As in the southern United States, where the "poor white," in
his hostility for the negro, entirely disregards the identity of economic interest, which he and his black fellow-worker have against
the land-owner and employer.

practical potency, it preaches a war of the poor against the rich; and, more than this, a war in which the poor are urged forward under the lash of envy, revenge, and covetousness. It preaches the kind of war that is no war, but a *jacquerie*.

This is not to say that Christianity cannot countenance the taking of strong measures by the community against functionless and predatory property, provided such measures are undertaken on behalf of the whole community, and in the spirit of service to it. But the Christian Faith of love and service cannot contemplate with anything but reprobation the indiscriminate turning loose upon any class, rich or not, of another class, hungering for vengeance and for spoil. The responsibility for the causes leading to the existence of such passions in the breasts of thousands of God's people is beside the point in this connection. It is enough here to point out the utter heathenishness of a creed which deliberately plays upon those passions. *God's Kingdom never will be built with the works of the devil.*

The doctrine of the materialistic conception of history has met less hostile criticism than the theories of the class-war and of capitalist accumulation, largely because most anti-socialists have not been themselves altogether free from materialism. There are two grounds upon which it has been commonly assailed: first, that it inoculates the Marxist with a deadening, optimistic fatalism; second, that it fixes his attention entirely on destruction.

In holding that the downfall of capitalism is as inevitable as the course of the sun, the materialistic conception of history gains in propagandist effect, for it inspires the Marxian revolutionary with an apocalyptic zeal. Yet it has a boomerang action, for the Marxist may well ask himself whether there is, after all, any need to do more than sit and gloat over the death agonies of the present order, while waiting for its final destruction before the inexorable advance of a new system. So it is that many Marxists have not merely refused to ally themselves with movements palliative of the present industrial regime, but have also withdrawn their badly needed aid from all efforts to end the evils of competition, which did not happen to proceed according to the precise schedule laid down in the pages of *Das Kapital*.[1] Again, the materialistic conception of history encourages the Marxist to concentrate his attention almost solely on the destructive aspect of social change. He has always prided himself on his insistence upon the uselessness of "Utopian" planning of a future society, whose form remains to be revealed by the inscrutable working of economic laws. Such an attitude may have had its uses in the days of Owenism and Fourierism. To-day it is damnable. It enables the Marxist merrily to go about the not uncongenial task of smashing the existing economic structure, without a thought of what is to follow, and all the time to dignify as "scientific" his policy of sabotaging civilization.

It is for the Christian sociologist, however, to lay down the most fundamental objection to this element of the Marxian formula. His position must be that of a categorical denial of the entire concept. Christianity and the Marxian interpretation of history are mutually incompatible. To believe that "man's ideas, views, and

[1] For example, the late Daniel de Leon, whose rigid Marxism forced him to withdraw his brilliant capacity and devoted courage from the American labour movement at a time when it was badly in need of both.

conceptions, in one word, man's consciousness, changes with every change in the conditions of his material existence, in his social relations and in his social life," is to believe something other than Christianity.[1] Such a theory not only contradicts the basis of Christian faith—and of any other spiritual outlook on life—it advances a thorough-going metaphysic of materialist absolutism; and being nothing but a sweeping speculation, it deserves no greater respect at the hands of Christian or other thinkers than that given to any piece of ambitious and unsubstantial abstraction.[2]

The Christian has, however, a more immediate objection to Marx's historical materialism than its metaphysics, and that is its ethics. A theory which declares that "the mode of production in material life determines the general character of the social, political, and spiritual processes of life"[3] amounts to a negation of any permanent moral values. In fact, it specifically ridicules religious and moral scruples towards its proposals as merely so many "bourgeois objections."[4] The practical significance of such a philosophy is startling. It is that any means to the proletarian revolution, and any conduct during or after it, are subject to no considerations save those of expediency. It means that the Marxist can do no wrong, because there is no right and no wrong.

It means that the bonds by which custom and religion hold men together, and restrain their brute instincts, may

[1] Marx and Engels, *op. cit.*, section 2.

[2] A complete discussion of the shortcomings of the theory as a complete philosophy of history may be found in Benedetto Croce, *Historical Materialism and the Economics of Karl Marx* (Macmillan translation). Cf. also Barth, *Philosophy of History as Sociology*.

[3] Marx, *Zur Kritik der Politiker Oekonomie*, Preface.

[4] Marx and Engels, *loc. cit.*

be lightly broken in the interests of the revolutionary programme. Chicane, intrigue, terror, may and do all find justification.

Together with the doctrine of the class-war, this aspect of Marxian materialism presents a sorry prospect for the future. The one arouses passions which Christianity has worked long centuries to overcome; the other invites the casting off of any checks on those passions.

The devoted disciple of Marx may reply: "The criticism of Marxism just made must be unfounded, for, otherwise, Marxism would have died long since. Must there not be something true and great in a theory which has retained its vigour undiminished despite a myriad of bitter attacks?" To this it must be replied that Marxism persists despite its logical fallacies and its appeal to the baser side of human nature, partly because of the half-truths it embodies, but mostly just because of its moral baseness.

Marxism, viewed historically, is little more than a systematic and imposingly learned statement of a set of ideas current in working-class movements for the past one hundred years, and it has received much of its strength because of this fact.

Most of the major doctrines of Marxism contain half-truths. Labour *is* an important element in value, although not its sole determinant. Capital *has* exploited labour through the wage contract, mercilessly and persistently, but there have been forms of exploitation of the worker, otherwise than through the wage contract, such as through rents, monopolies, adulterated goods, and jerry-built houses. The warfare between labour and capital *has* profoundly affected the history of the world, since the industrial revolution, but it is not the only class-conflict which that era has witnessed, and has not always been the most important.

Nevertheless, to the working-man, wage exploitation, and the battle against the employing class have been the most obvious forms in which his sufferings and his struggles have taken form; so that he has magnified their importance. Naturally, therefore, he has listened gladly to a doctrine that has over-emphasized these features.

As for the theory of labour-value, this was generally accepted by "orthodox" economists as well as revolutionists at the time the working-class movement began to become articulate.[1] Moreover, it has probably been at the back of revolutionary ideology for centuries, as a result of the teachings of the mediæval Church.[2]

The Marxian theory of value has therefore merely formulated what working-men were believing at the time it was first propounded, and have mistakenly clung to ever since, while the doctrine of the class-struggle draws its vitality from psychological rather than historical sources, as has already been shown. It may further be pointed out that the first collisions of labour against capital occurred at a time when an age-long series of conflicts between social classes was reaching its climax, and when the economic and social alignments were often identical. It has, accordingly, been natural for the modern economic struggle to echo the phrases and the emotional atmosphere of the earlier social conflicts, and also for the worker to continue to identify all antagonisms with economic ones.

[1] Beer, *History of British Socialism*, vol. i. part ii. chap. ii. pp. 209-234. Cf. also the history and literature of the Chartist period.

[2] O'Brien, *Mediæval Economic Teaching*, pp. 65-67; Ingram, *History of Political Economy*, second edition, p. 27; Haney, *History of Economic Thought*, second edition, p. 92.

In sum, Marxism was given to the world at a time
when the working-classes already held most of the
theories it contained. And it has continued popular
because it has confirmed their belief in the jumble of fact
and fancy found in such ideas, rather than attempt the
unpopular task of telling them the truth.[1]

Nevertheless, if these were the only circumstances
favourable to the acceptance of the Marxian formulas,
one might expect their popularity gradually to diminish.
The effects of the historical coincidences which made the
launching of Marxism propitious are fading out; and the
clouds of confused thinking in the labour movement
are gradually being dispelled. Yet Marxism shows few
signs of abatement. It has continued strong, because the
chief source of its vigour has been of a sort which social
change and intellectual enlightenment cannot effect. *The
principal strength of Marxism has been its moral
weakness.*

The heart of Marxism is the class-war.[2] The economic
analysis gives to it an unsubstantial appearance of
scientific authoritativeness; the materialistic conception
of history endows it with an encouraging reassurance of
success. But they are both subordinate to it. They can
be, and have been, discredited; yet the creed of the class-
war carries on.

Why it does so has already been made clear. The
class-war is an unholy war. Its motives are envy and

[1] It may well be asked whether Marx was anything more than
the exponent of the theories current at his time: a sort of scholastic
of Chartism. Cf. Beer, *op. cit.* vol. ii. p. 214, and *Karl Marx, sein
Leben und sein Lehren*, p. 34, and Marx's "Speech on Free Trade,"
in Appendix to the Kerr translation of *La Misère de la Philosophe*.

[2] As mild a Socialist as John Spargo acknowledges "the class-
struggle as the central *motif* of modern Socialism." Spargo, *Applied
Socialism*, p. 115.

greed and blind revenge. Its weapons are trickery and terror and brute force. Its philosophy is the deliberate denial of morality. Its objective is mere destruction.

And all of this appeals to men—particularly men hungry and hopeless and oppressed by a stupid and heedless governing class. It appeals to them because no man—God forgive him—is very far out of the jungle, and because such as they especially have been driven back upon their brute selves by a society which has persistently thwarted their human personality. Treated little better than savages, they have heeded the call of the Marxian class-war to act as they have been treated, and to rend civilization by a new barbarian invasion from out of its own slums.

It is for the Christian to show them "a more excellent way." It is for him to bring them the aid of all men of good will, in making them not less, but more human, that they may enter into their inheritance in the Kingdom of God.

THE KINGDOM OF GOD AND THE CHURCH TO-DAY

FATHER PAUL B. BULL

Priest of the Community of the Resurrection, Mirfield

Author of *The Sacramental Principle*, etc.

SYNOPSIS

1. The disease of our age is disintegration of human life due to organization apart from God.

2. Synthesis. Christ is the only bond which can bind men together as He is the basis of our Humanity.

3. The ideal of the Church is not to guarantee salvation, but to be God's agent in redemption, to establish God's Kingdom among men.

4. The Church to-day has lost the millions because she has failed to sanctify politics and economics through a pietistic and individualistic interpretation of the Gospel. The causes of her failure may be summarized under these heads.

   (i.) *Idolatry.* She has acquiesced in the depersonalization of labour and in the unrestrained covetousness which makes an Idol of Money. The unjust accumulation of financial power cannot be moralized. The official utterances of Church authorities are admirable theoretically but practically ineffectual. The idolatry of property, power, and pleasure makes Christian teaching ineffectual.

   (ii.) *Sectionalism.* The divorce of prayer and worship from economic life leaves the greater part of human life unsanctified. This applies to nominal Catholicism as well as to Puritanism. The making of a soul. This sectionalism is a debasement of Catholic ideals and accounts for the loss of many to the Church.

   (iii.) *Selfishness.* Atomic personality has disintegrated the Fellowship of the Church.

5. The Remedy is to return to the unity of the Faith as referring both the life of the individual and of society to God. Belief in Christ alone preserves human values. The Catholic complex of dogma, discipline, and devotion alone preserves the social principles of the Gospel, Faith, Freedom, and Fellowship.

CHAPTER IX

THE KINGDOM OF GOD AND THE CHURCH TO-DAY

THE preceding essays of this volume have shown by searching criticism that the present organization of industry and our economic life is defective and doomed to disaster for lack of a co-ordinating spiritual principle to bind them into a rational whole; and that the Kingdom of God is that principle which alone can weave up the life of man into a perfect synthesis. The object of this essay is to ask how far the Church is fulfilling its purpose of founding the Kingdom of God on earth; and to suggest the principles which should penetrate and rule our social and economic life when it is dominated by the thought of the reign of Christ.

I. DISINTEGRATION.

If we ask what is the root of the disease from which our civilization is suffering, in my judgment the answer may be given in the one word—Disintegration. The attempt to organize the life of man apart from God has deprived us of the only bond which can bind mankind together. The attempt to interpret the universe exclusively by one or the other term of the sacramental principles has led to the divorce of what God has joined together. The divorce of the outward material form from its inward spiritual principle may be seen in every activity of our life. In economics the disintegration began when the labourer was divorced from the land. The landless labourer inevitably becomes a wage-slave. The wage-system divorces the labour-power from the labourer, and depersonalizes and dehumanizes industry. So wealth is divorced from the work which produces it; work divorced from the worship which should consecrate it; property divorced from the function which alone justifies it, and the community which should be knit together by bonds of mutual service is disintegrated into warring classes and competing individuals.

In education and study over-specialization too often divorces science from art, thought from feeling, the head from the heart, so that a mental disintegration leads to a false valuation of life, that cash valuation of spiritual gifts and opportunities which establishes plutocracy. We seem to be in real peril of gaining the whole world and losing our true life if our industrial organization merely multiplies commodities while character decays.

This disintegration of human life begins in the individualistic interpretation of our Faith on the false basis of a discredited atomic philosophy; which by ignoring the social and sacramental aspect of religion divorces the spiritual from the material, the soul from the body, the individual from society, and society from God.

II. Synthesis.

We believe that in Christ alone, the eternal Son of God, who unites in His own Person the natures of God and man: the Son of Man, because in each person He is the basis of our common humanity, in Him alone can be found a common human basis and that objective reference and standard of values which will give to men a common aim, and that spirit of fellowship which will bind the nations into one. St. Paul speaks of Him as the One "in whom all things consist" or hold together: and it is just that bond of unity which can alone redeem us from an ever-increasing disintegration. Society must have some unifying principle. Based on selfishness alone society is dead, and in time must fall to pieces and become like worms crawling away from a decaying corpse, instead of like cells, each making its best contribution to a living body.

III. THE IDEAL OF THE CHURCH.

Man can only be redeemed from selfishness by being incorporated into a divine and human fellowship, and so while our Lord says so little about the salvation of the individual soul, He trained and educated and disciplined His Apostles to found this Divine Society. The Christian method of redemption is primarily corporate. It begins with the descent of the Holy Spirit on the day of Pentecost, which united the Apostles into a Divine and human Fellowship. Until this Fellowship was formed by the descent of the Holy Spirit, individual effort to evangelize was forbidden. When the Fellowship of the divine humanity was created individual souls were added to it (Acts ii. 47).

The Church was formed to be the Body of Christ, through which He would continue to energize, to carry on through the ages those things that He began "both to do and to teach" in His life on earth (Acts i. 1). His last discourses echoed the first trumpet call of His ministry: for He came preaching the Gospel of the Kingdom, and after His resurrection for forty days He appeared to them "speaking the things concerning the Kingdom of God." The Church was formed to be His agent in the redemption of the world, to establish the Kingdom of

God, to incorporate men into His divine humanity, to bind them together in the Fellowship of the Holy Spirit, in order that in a brotherhood knit together by love His life might be manifested, His teaching proclaimed, and His work fulfilled.

The first necessity is that the Church should have the mind of Christ. This mind of Christ will include an abiding consciousness of God the Father, that faith which is the instinctive reference of all things to God. The Church finds in God the Father the shrine of the absolute values of Righteousness and Justice, Truth and Freedom which are the very foundations of the Throne of God, and the only possible bonds for the Brotherhood of man. And in Christ she finds the revelation of all values, human and divine, which gives stability to her moral judgments. Each soul will be infinitely precious to the Church because he is dear to the Father as a child of God and redeemed by the love of Christ. This relationship of Father and Son is the governing principle of the economics of the Kingdom of God. It is imperative and supreme. It proclaims and preserves the priceless value of each human being. It fixes his relationship to all other men as that of Brothers. It condemns selfishness and unrestrained competition, the crude animal appeal to brute force which cannot be tolerated in a family. It is the basis of Christian ethics which are founded on the two great commandments in their threefold reference: "Thou shalt love the Lord thy God with all thy heart and all thy mind, with all thy soul and all thy strength. And thou shalt love thy neighbour as thyself." The mind of Christ in His Church will insist that man's life is Theo-centric and not ego-centric: that the one and only basis of human society is relationship to God.

The mind of Christ will inflame the Church with an undying passion for the coming of the Kingdom of Heaven among men. It will inspire the Church with a passion for redemption. For the Church was not formed to be the sphere of a guaranteed salvation, but the living co-operative agent of redemption. As long as man is an incarnate spirit the Church must minister to him on the sacramental principle. It will have a threefold life, institutional, ethical, and mystical, corresponding to man's body, soul, and spirit. But as long as it has the mind of Christ it will subordinate the institutional to the ethical, and base the ethical on the mystical, the union with God by love. The history of the Church suggests that when she has exalted the institutional aspect of her life above the ethical, or allowed the ethical to be divorced from the mystical, morals from religion, she has failed in her mission as surely as a man's life becomes disordered if his bodily impulses are indulged without moral restraint, or if his moral nature loses its imperative by ignoring God. If the Church is truly possessed by the Spirit of Christ she will proclaim fearlessly the absolute supremacy of God, the priceless value of each human life, the iniquity of every sin against brotherhood; and, regardless of consequences, she will fling down her challenge to the world by exposing every falsehood, by denouncing class privilege and vested interest. She will claim her right to be crucified with Christ, if she desires to live with His life and share in His victory.

IV. THE CHURCH TO-DAY.

Are we satisfied with the witness of the Church to-day? Is she really fulfilling her function of establishing the Kingdom of God on earth? Why was she unable to avert the bloody war among nations nominally Christian? Why are Christians unable to cope with the industrial chaos and floods of immorality which have come to a crisis in the War? Why has the Church of England lost its hold on the millions? Why are nonconformist bodies also failing? Why is the nation growing up apart from God? The facts are no longer in dispute. Not one per cent. of the men of the nation are regular communicants. In one workshop in a northern town of seventy-eight men, only five ever set foot in a place of worship. In a district in London advantage was taken of the conscription census to ascertain the religious allegiance of boys from fourteen to eighteen years of age. Of 12,500 boys between these ages, including Jews and Roman Catholics, only 2,300 professed to belong to any religious body. This means that in one district of one city, over 10,000 boys are not connected with any religious body whatever. The communicants in several dioceses in England are not 6 per cent. of the population. "Twenty-six million children and youths in the United States are growing up without any systematic training in religion" (*Religion and Business*, p. 132, R. W. Babson, President of the Babson Statistical Organization). I could multiply this evidence a thousand-fold if space permitted, but this must suffice.

Here, then, is the symptom. What is the cause of the disease, and how can it be cured? The Church has lost the millions because clergy have been content to deal with symptoms without attempting to remove the cause of the disease.

May we not summarize the cause thus? That a false presentation of Christianity has disintegrated Christendom, and left vast forces which largely control the life of man unconsecrated to the service of God. The evil tradition, which is not yet abandoned, that Christianity has nothing to do with politics and economics has banished God from 95 per cent. of the life of man. For politics and economics regulate homes, housing, schools, education, wages, sanitation, industry, and commerce, with all the relationships which these involve. If this 95 per cent. of the life of the people is dissociated from God and religion, what wonder is it if they feel that God doesn't count in the battle of life.

We cannot, if we believe in God, ignore the past without imperilling the future. We have to face the black record of the officials of the Church since the commencement of the Industrial Revolution from 1760 onward, as faithfully revealed in such admirable books as the Hammond's *Village, Town,* and *Skilled Labourer.* If only the Church people will face the past, repent and confess it, and resolve to amend their lives, God is ready to forgive. Already there are signs of a new stirring of the Spirit of God in the hearts of men. The sins which have paralysed the Church in the immediate past may, in my judgment, be summed up under the heads of Idolatry, Sectionalism, and Selfishness.

1. IDOLATRY.

The Church, by which in this Essay is generally meant the prevailing opinion of Christian people, has acquiesced in that Covetousness which St. Paul describes as idolatry. Her formulated teaching is irreproachable. Every child in her schools is taught in her catechism "not to covet or desire other men's goods. . . ." He is, then, at the age of fourteen sent out into an industrial and commercial world, whose life is based on the acquisitive instinct, whose methods are those of unrestrained com-

petition, the law of the Jungle, the survival of the fittest,
which in this case often means the most cunning and
unscrupulous. However, we are not concerned with
formulæ but with prevailing opinion. The first step in
idolatry was to depersonalize the labourer by rendering
him landless, and then detaching from him his labour-
force; so that in starting a business a man buys so much
raw material and machinery, so many volts of electricity,
and so much man-power or labour-force. Under the
wage-slavery of landless men the old intimate personal
relationships between employers and employed has dis-
appeared, the labourer is robbed of his personality and
becomes Labour, an abstraction, a mere impersonal
force to be manipulated for the purposes of other men,
cannon-fodder in war, mammon-fodder in peace, an
instrument for the ends of other persons. Having de-
personalized the labourer, our industrial system seems
to have endowed Money with the personality. When
the War had reached a certain stage we were told that
"Money began to talk," "Money is shy," "Money is
very tight!" "Money breeds Money," and a brood of
deadly vices, and at last mounts the throne of God as
Mammon, and in the form of Property, Pleasure, and
Power claims and wins the adoration of the world.
Mammon-worship destroys the soul by the trans-valu-
ation of all values into terms of cash, the cash valuation
of spiritual gifts and opportunities. Thus Feudalism
is converted into Plutocracy by defiling the fountain of
honour with the sale of titles. This cash valuation of
spiritual gifts and opportunities pervades all life and
degrades it. It consecrates itself in the phrase "the
sacred rights of property." Money gives power. It
affords pleasure. It inflames selfish ambition. It gives

or withholds the higher education. It controls the lives of millions in the labour market by giving or withholding credit, and so manipulating employment and unemployment. It bribes or crushes every opponent. It controls the legislature. It penalizes virtue. It commercializes vice. It makes desolating war and sordid peace. It corrupts and stifles the conscience, and drugs and deadens the soul.

Karl Marx was wrong in prophesying the concentration of "capital" in fewer and fewer hands. The rise of limited liability companies falsified this prophesy. But his instinct was not at fault. The effectual control of commerce and industry, of opportunity and freedom, has become concentrated into the hands of a few immensely powerful trusts and groups of international financiers who control governments, and make peace and war: and who frequently in times of crisis are themselves unable to restrain the vast forces they manipulate.

Can the Church moralize this vast force of accumulated financial power and consecrate it to the fulfillment of God's Will? No, in my judgment, she cannot. It is born of an unjust distribution of the rewards of labour, and it rests on an immoral basis of functionless property. What can she do? Nothing at all so long as Christian people (with many noble exceptions) are given up to that idolatry which is covetousness. If they return to God, they can regulate the distribution of the rewards of labour on righteous principles, and establish property on the moral basis of function instead of force. But this means an entire change of mind, a true repentance, if the Kingdom of God is to come in our commercial and industrial life. The Church, by withdrawing from the political and economic spheres has lost its power to consecrate them. It is fatally easy and obviously profitable to accept the fact of wealth without asking how riches are acquired or how they are spent. Thus, from the break up of the unity of Christendom till quite recently, the Church has offered Christians no guidance as to justice and righteousness in accumulating riches, and suggested no limit to selfish expenditure on luxury.

Was Karl Marx or Bismarck right? The first said that "Religion is opium for the people." The second describes Christianity as a revolutionary force so dangerous that it must be controlled by the State. Both statements are partly true. Christianity as preached by Jesus Christ is undoubtedly a revolutionary force. Religion as controlled by the power of wealth which "tunes the pulpit," is a mere sedative, a drug. But it is not Christianity. Would it not be more true to say that religion is opium for the rich? As preached in many fashionable churches it drugs the conscience, it darkens the mind, it deadens the heart.

Mr. Roger W. Babson, in describing the average New England small town, writes words which are equally true in a more subtle form of many a village and town in old England: "There is the mill which furnishes employment to most of the people: there is the great house on the hill in which the owner of the mill lives: and there is the local church in which the mill-owner is the largest contributor and often the leading officer. In most instances this man has been a real benefit to the community, and in many cases he is quite sincere and fairly unselfish. In many instances, however, he is looked upon as a hard-hearted skinflint. He often has mortgages on many of the homes: he perhaps has a bad record as to the treatment of his labour (note the abstraction) and he is generally feared if not hated by towns-people. The Church suffers from such men. Not only do they dominate the minister and make life miserable for him, but they bring reproach on the whole Church industry. . . . Not content with running their own business and a good part of the town, these men are determined to run the Church and the preacher" (*Religion and Business,* p. 13). Multiply this by many millions and we shall understand how difficult it is for institutional religion to resist the pressure of high finance.

The Christian bodies in America have issued an admirable Report on "Christianity and Industry," even excelling in courage and clearness the excellent Report issued by the Archbishops' Committee on the same subject in England. But are these solemn utterances of the leaders of Religion, these efforts to proclaim the principles which should sanctify our economic arrangements, accepted by Christian people? Scarcely at all, I fear. The poor welcome the proclamation of these Christian principles. In Glasgow, a labour leader read out twelve propositions on property to a meeting of communists and extreme socialists. Each proposition was greeted with enthusiastic cheers by this revolutionary audience. The speaker then said: "These propositions are taken verbatim from the Archbishops' Report on 'Christianity and Industry,' as the teaching of Jesus Christ. So don't let us hear any more about Religion being opium for the people."

On the other hand, when in two fashionable Churches in England the declaration of the 350 Anglican bishops on the same subject was made the subject of a course of sermons by two eloquent preachers, one course was brought to an abrupt conclusion by the remonstrances of "the faithful" who will not tolerate any criticism of unearned increment and vested interests which is likely to be effectual. In the other case, the audience gradually

faded away, with indignant mutterings of "Socialism"
and "sheer Bolshevism." Truly as of old "the common
people heard Him gladly"; but the rulers said: "He
stirreth up the people." This sheer idolatry of property,
power, and pleasure, of comfort, luxury, and influence,
which makes men refuse to listen to any effectual criticism of profits, dividends, and rent has established
a silent tyranny over the ministry. Heavy institutional
commitments make the Church too dependent on the
favour of the wealthy. The priest who too faithfully
echoes his Master's teaching will not be crucified: but his
work will be starved, he will be frozen out with the
polite and polished warning that, "unless he is more tact-
ful he will certainly imperil his promotion." Through
the disastrous association with the State, which places
much of the patronage of the Church in the hands of
politicians, it is easy to understand how the flames of
Pentecost may be trimmed to illuminate a garden party
of respectability, and how the bride of Christ may become
the concubine of Caesar. But the evil is not merely due
to State alliance. It is due to an evil economic system.
It is as common among Non-conformists as in the Church
of England. Several of the Labour Members of Parliament have once been local preachers whose bold criticism
of what is unrighteous and unjust in our present system,
awakened the fears and hostility of the wealthy members
of their denominations, and of the officials who dispensed
with their services. So would they drive Christ from
their Churches and Chapels if He imperilled vested
interests by His teaching. The future of the Church
depends on the degree of self-sacrifice and zeal with
which wealthy Christians hasten to moralize their
property and humanize their industry, forsaking idols
and restoring personality to Labour, that the image of

God may once more shine forth from a brother's face who co-operates with freedom and fellowship in work for the commonwealth.

2. SECTIONALISM.

When we ask how has this widespread idolatry arisen, we may possibly find the answer in the prevalance of sectionalism among Christians, the habit of divorcing what God has joined together. It is not confined to religion. It infects every department of thought. Over-specialization and excessive differentiation isolate one branch of knowledge from another, and lead to mental disintegration, a loss of proportion in the judgment. The wide application of the scientific method emphasizes this disintegration. For nothing is more common than to find men of science making an abstraction for the purpose of study, and then mistaking the truth of this abstraction for the truth of the whole. But here we must confine ourselves to sectionalism in the Church to-day, and note how it divorces what God has joined together. The teaching of the Puritan, who neglects to sanctify the material universe by a false spirituality which ignores the body, works out in a denial of the Incarnation; and the Catholic who fails to consecrate the economic life by concentrating all attention on a merely "sanctuary" religion, is equally guilty of divorcing what God has joined together. Souls are not *made* apart from the body; nor are they made in the Sanctuary merely by Prayer and Sacraments. These are their strength and joy and crown. The Sanctuary is the power-station of their life, reinforcing every activity of their soul. But souls are *made* in the strain and stress of daily life, in home and school, factory, in office, mill and workshop, wherever a child has to think or will or love, their souls are made, as between right and wrong, good and evil, the shuttle of the will moves ceaselessly backward and forward weaving the web of character. The soul is evolved in the strain of conflict as the one primitive innate instinct, the will to live, is educated into the will to live *with* others, which with increasing responsibility grows into the will to live *for* others: and when this is perfected by a readiness to die for others the will to live has become the will to love, and the soul is made. For to love is to live; and there is no other life.

If this be a true account of the formation of character and the making of a soul, it will at once be realized that the economic relationships in commerce and industry are as spiritual and important as prayer or Bible-reading, Mass and Sacraments. The Puritan who confines his conception of spirituality to his thoughts about God and himself, to what he calls his soul's life, is profoundly mistaken. The very things he despises or fails to consecrate—beauty, art, music, movement, colour, architecture, science, and industry—are often far more spiritual than his opinion about predestination and election: for true art is the living embodiment of creative personality and the expression of the absolute values of the good, the beautiful, and the true—a real unveiling of God which purifies and stimulates the soul: while many theological discussions are merely the expression of man's perversity. The Puritan's failure to consecrate the material universe is due to his loss of the sacramental principle. He divorces what God has joined together, the material and the spiritual, the body and the soul. This utterly false spirituality has no warrant in the Bible, and no justification in the Christian religion. For the Bible teaches the consecration of art and craft and labour to God in a vocational industry. "And the Lord spake unto Moses, saying, See I have called by name Bezal-eel. . . and have filled him with the Spirit of God, in wisdom and in understanding and in knowledge, and in all manner of workmanship, to devise cunning works, to work in gold and in silver and in brass, and in cutting of stones for setting, and in carving of wood to work in all manner of workmanship" (Exodus xxxi. 2). While the consecration of all honest labour into which we put our heart as an acceptable sacrifice to God is proclaimed in these words: "They will maintain the fabric of the world: and in the handiwork of their craft is their prayer" (Ecclus. xxxviii. 34).

The same Sectionalism may be observed among a section of clergy who call themselves Catholic, but have little right to such a noble name. For they preach a merely "sanctuary" religion of Confession and Mass entirely dissociated from the social and economic life of the people. But to dissociate sacraments and sacrifice and worship from the social and economic life of the people is to pervert worship by divorcing what God has joined together. The Sacraments are essentially social, the action of the Divine Fellowship of God and man in the Holy Catholic Church. A man confesses to his priest because his sins are not a matter between his soul and God alone, but by them he has injured the Brotherhood of the Baptized, the Divine Fellowship, the body of Christ. The priest judges his penitence and absolves him in God's name, because he is set apart by God for this function in the life of the Fellowship. The whole Body of the Church is a priestly body, the Body of our great High Priest, who has ordained the ministerial priesthood to fulfil this function of the body, to restore the penitent to full communion in the Divine Fellowship.

The priest offers the Holy Sacrifice of the Mass because God in the Fellowship has set him apart to fulfil this function of the Body. His action is not the private act of an individual, but the corporate action of the Fellowship. In the Mass he does not merely offer the sinless humanity of Christ to the Father in isolation from the faithful. This would be to offer the Head without the Body. At every mass Christ is offered in all the fulness of redeemed Humanity. The whole material universe which He created and which only consists (or holds together) in Him, is represented by the bread and wine and water: the whole human race, for whom He died, in whom He lives, are represented by the little band of faithful who have responded to His call, and whom He has incorporated by Holy Baptism into His Divine Humanity, to be His body through whom He may work out the redemption of the world. They labour for Him. He works in them. They work and suffer and witness for Him in home and office, mill and mine, throughout the week; and on the Lord's day they bring their offering, all that they have said and done, every effort of honest work, all that they have done or suffered, they bring their sacrifice of service to Christ that He may cleanse it, and make it His own, and offer it to the Father. The sacrifice of Christ which redeemed the world was the entire consecration of His human nature to the service of God the Father in the task of establishing God's Kingdom on earth. He offered throughout His life the perfect response of body, soul, and spirit, of heart and mind and will to the Will of God the Father. This is what He still offers in every Eucharist. But now, His sacred humanity has won a vast extension. For every soul baptized into the Church becomes a member of Christ, a partaker of the divine nature, and a part of

His living body, the Church. In these, His members, Christ penetrates into every home and factory, mine and mill. In them He offers Himself to the Father for His service. Through them He ceaselessly witnesses for righteousness and justice. Through them He labours for the coming of the Kingdom. It is this Body of Christ, consecrated men and women whom He has incorporated body and soul into His Divine Humanity in the Fellowship of the Catholic Church, that our great High Priest offers to the Father in every Eucharist.

As surely as the bread and wine become the most holy Body and the most precious Blood of Christ, and also by devout communion become the body and blood of the Christian, so surely does Christ offer Himself in all the fulness of redeemed humanity, that is to say, in the Church which is His Body, to the Father. "I in them, and Thou in me, that they may be perfected into one."

Now to isolate one aspect of the holy sacrifice from the other, to separate the Body and Blood of Christ in the Blessed Sacrament from the members of Christ in the Church; to adore Him in the tabernacle on the Altar and to fail to recognize Him in the starving child in the slums, in whom He dwells, whose body He has consecrated to be His tabernacle, the shrine of Diety, where God delights to dwell; to find Christ in the Sanctuary and to miss Him in the workshop, is that spirit of sectionalism or schism which makes so much nominal Catholicism futile and worthless. The only true Catholicism claims the whole life of every man for God, body, soul and spirit, in home and school, in factory, mine, and workshop. Therefore it must raise an unceasing protest against an unchristian organization of commerce and industry, which ignores God, and destroys His image in man.

Why is so much noble and courageous spiritual effort by our parish priests utterly wasted? Why are they often heartbroken at the spiritual apathy of their flock? Is it not because their efforts are misdirected, and because that in tolerating an unchristian organization of indus- try they are shirking the real battle with evil. They send their children out to fight a foe whom they have never fought themselves. The boy and girl at fourteen years of age, with the glow of their confirmation fresh upon them, are sent out to spend the greater part of their daily life in an atmosphere of materialism from which every spiritual value has been eliminated. This godless, soul- less, inhuman, impersonal, mechanical system of indus- try bleeds them white of all true vitality by exhausting toil. It destroys their sense of beauty to which God would appeal in His revelation of Himself. It disin- tegrates the family. It has destroyed home life. It lowers every high ideal. It deadens every activity of the soul. It destroys every spiritual value. Boy after boy comes back to his friend wounded and bleeding from his first brave battle to preserve his honour and integrity and truthfulness in business with the bitter cry, "It is impos- sible to be a Christian in business."

We do not forget the noble efforts of many business men to sanctify this system. But it is impossible really to sanctify what is wrong in principle, and an economic based solely on the acquisitive instinct and the unre- strained selfishness of the individual cannot be made to serve God's purpose.

So we say to our brethren in the ministry: 'Why do you complain of apathy and indifference when you toler- ate a materialistic organization of industry which stifles the souls of men? Why don't you issue forth from the sanctuary, and carry your Gospel of Divine Humanity into the workshop where the battle is being fought? You are right in believing that in the Catholic Faith is the only hope for the redemption of mankind. But you are wrong in narrowing your Catholicism to the sanctuary and the home. No religion is catholic which does not claim the whole of the life of every man and of all mankind—domestic, industrial, commercial, national, international, and ecclesiastical for God: and the future as well as the past. It is not enough to grope about with canonists and antiquarians among the grave-clothes of the past, with a merely backward look, as though the Holy Spirit had left the Church some centuries ago. We must try to seize the opportunity of the future. We must change the Catholicism of the Tombs for the Catholicism of the Mountain-tops, with its world-wide vision, and a heart on fire with missionary zeal and social enthusiasm.

3. SELFISHNESS.

We may note in every department of life the interaction of two principles which modify one another—in our method of knowledge, the intellectual and mystical, the knowledge of the head and of the heart, in our religious conceptions, the reaction of the ideal and the practical, and in our political theory the reaction of the individual and society. Human life seems best symbolized by an ellipse with two foci, and best interpreted by the swing of the pendulum between these two points of the individual and the social aspects of life. Ideas undoubtedly rule the world, but the world reacts on and modifies the ideas. The Church starts out to convert the world: the world largely succeeds in converting the Church. Man invents machinery to serve him in his work, and awakens to find himself the slave of his machine. There is then an incessant action and reaction of spirit and matter, of body and soul, of religious and philosophic ideas on the economic life, and of economic conditions on religious beliefs.

So when at the Renaissance ideas proved too strong for the crushing intellectual tyranny of the Papacy, the pendulum of the human mind swung from the rigid despotism of the Papacy to the equally false extreme of the unrestrained individualism of Protestantism. The atomic conception of personality which treats each man as a separate, independent, isolated individual, formulated itself in such expressions as that, "My religion is between myself and God alone." "I don't want anyone between my soul and God." "Religion has nothing to do with economics and politics." This exaggerated individualism is of course in clear contradiction to the Christian Faith which is the Gospel of the Kingdom, the bond of a Fellowship. It practically denies the whole method of our redemption. Christ redeems man from that selfishness which is the essence of sin by incorporating him into a Brotherhood. Man can only save his life by losing it in a fellowship of mutual service.

This false religious individualism, based on the fallacy of atomic personality, has substituted the selfish conception of a merely individual salvation for the corporate redemption, which Christ came to preach; and personal pietism has been substituted for social righteousness— "Is your soul saved?" for "Thy Kingdom come as in heaven so on earth." This religious heresy inevitably expresses itself in an economic fallacy. The exaggerated individualism of Protestantism shattered the unity of Christendom, and left the vast forces of economic and social life uncontrolled by a common purpose. In the Middle Ages, in spite of every glaring defect, the life of man was a unity and a community knit together by the bond of a common Faith. The same reference to God which inspired his personal devotion, also controlled and regulated his social and economic relationships. The town or village was a community, with a common Faith, common lands, corporate work in Guilds. Industry was vocational, a social function of the common life. Property rested on a functional basis, some useful duty done for the commonwealth. But with the break-up of Christendom, the principle of disruption which shattered its religious life expressed itself in economic disintegration. The spirit which said, "My religion is between my soul and God alone," was translated into economic terms, "A man can do what he likes with his own." As religion ignored brotherhood in egoistic self-assertion so industry ceased to be regarded as a social function, and took as its motive the unrestrained accumulation of private profit for the individual in entire disregard of the commonwealth. The Church came to be regarded as an aggregation of pious individuals who for personal benefit agreed to worship together, instead of a family and fellowship bound together by the bond of a common partaking of the life of God in Christ. The sacraments have come to be regarded only as means for the strengthening of the individual soul instead of the corporate expression of that fellowship with one another based on fellowship with God in His Son Jesus Christ.

Thus a disintegrated Christendom leads to a disintegrated economic and social life, and our one and only hope of redemption lies in the return of Christ to reign over us, and once more to bind us together in a Brotherhood of the Common Life, to restore the unity which selfishness has shattered.

V. The Remedy.

The appalling character of the late War and the sordid nature of the Peace have forced thoughtful men to consider whether it is possible to redeem an economic system based on the unrestrained selfishness of the individual, under which the labourer has lost his personal value and become mere mechanical force, and industry has lost its divine purpose as communal service and sacrifice, and become slavery. For the essence of slavery is to use man as an instrument for the ends of other men when God created him as an end in himself. The unrestrained competition of individualism leads inevitably to the suicide of the human race in a world-wide war. A collectivism which ignores the freedom of the individual kills initiative and enterprise, degenerates into bureaucracy, and perishes in stagnation. The hope of redemption lies in the threefold reference of the Catholic Faith, by which both the individual and corporate life while they react on one another are harmonized and kept healthy by being brought into relationship with God. As against the depersonalization and demoralization of human life and values which inevitably occurs when man is dissociated from God, we believe that the redemption of man can only come by a return to God who created him for Himself, made him in His own image, whose love for him gives him his real value, and only in communion with whom can those human values be preserved.

Now this threefold reference of the individual to the corporate life, and of both to God, is laid down by our Lord as the basis of the Christian religion. "Thou shalt love the Lord thy God with all thy heart and mind and soul and strength, and thy neighbour as thyself." And it is interesting to note that in the Athanasian Creed we have the rich development of this threefold reference,

and find the true principles of human society enshrined
in the very nature of God the ever-blessed Trinity, which
gives to our socialism its rock-like spiritual foundation.
Our Lord's analysis of human nature, which seems to
us final and absolute as the basis of social philosophy,
may be summed up in three propositions: (1) That the
individual is of infinite and priceless value, (2) That
he can only realize himself by self-sacrifice; can only
save his life by losing it in a larger synthesis in service
for the commonwealth. (3) That this realization of the
individual in the corporate life of fellowship can only
be harmonized by the reference of both individual and
corporate life to God and to His Will.

This is the image of God in man. The doctrine of
the Ever Blessed Trinity preserves Individuality in Fellowship, "neither confounding the Persons, nor dividing
the substance." It recognizes a functional activity of the
Fellowship—Father, Son, and Holy Ghost, each standing for a definite activity, and all co-operating in the
work of each. It recognizes an equality of status which
is not inconsistent with a precedence of function. The
Son is "equal to the Father as touching his Godhead, and
inferior to the Father as touching His manhood." In
industry this preserves the differentiation of function
essential to corporate effort in authority, management,
direction, and planning as communal functions, and
saves them from becoming a caste distinction. The union
of God and Man in the Incarnation of the eternal
Son of God when interpreted into terms of industry
secures for us that all that is truly human shall be
regarded as really divine. It saves us from that fatal
schism between secular and sacred: it consecrates industry to be a holy sacrifice: it humanizes worship to be a
social activity. Through Christ it preserves in every

man the human and the divine in the unity of personality
—"one, not by the conversion of the Godhead into flesh,"
as in the philosophy of Humanitarians and some Modernists, "but by the taking of the Manhood into God,"
as in the Catholic sacraments. "One altogether; not by
confusion of substance, but by unity of Person. For
as the reasonable soul and flesh is one man, so God and
Man is one Christ." Here is the eternal protest of God
and His Church against our present system, which
mangles human personality by scientific abstractions:
which treats a Son of God who works with his
hands as a mere "hand," a supplier of labour-force,
and ignores his personality, his pride in work, his creative impulse, his affections, his family relationships, his
spiritual character.

Nor would I surrender one word of the damnatory
clauses if only the Creed be translated from its original
purpose of a defensive philosophic statement of the
Faith, and given its social significance. Without this
Catholic Faith firmly held, which bases social relationship
on Fellowship with God, Society cannot be saved. Without this reference of all ends and purposes to God's Will
and to the absolute values of Justice and Righteousness,
human values cannot be preserved. There is nothing
wrong in damning or condemning, if you damn the right
things. In our decadent civilization men damn the wrong
things. But Plutocracy in its destruction of every spiritual value, in its trampling on personality in that unrestrained competition which is inevitably plunging the
world into another world-wide war, in the coarse bru-
tality which blackens and blots out every beauty of
nature in the making of private profits, till the power
to appreciate beauty is perishing from the soul of our
people, this system which destroys the true life of our

people in the effort to get a living, is altogether damnable. Is is not just because the Church damns the wrong persons, that she has lost influence with the people? Fifty years ago the official Church launched all the thunders of the Church and State against a few clergy who wore vestments; and with the consent of the Bishops, priests were actually flung into prison for this supposed offence, while the officials of the Church were steadily indifferent to social righteousness and justice. If the Athanasian Creed be given a social interpretation its damnatory causes are much needed for sweaters, profiteers, and for those international financiers, who have called into existence an inhuman power which they themselves are unable to control, which threatens to kindle the everlasting fires of greed and hostility and hatred and incessant war among men, and to make human life a hell on earth.

The application of the Catholic Faith to our industrial and economic life may be summed up in the three words: Faith, Freedom and Fellowship. Faith in God and man gives the spiritual basis of social life, and preserves human values. Freedom secures initiative, creative enterprise, and the full expansion of Personality; and Fellowship, which makes industry a communal effort for the commonwealth, corrects the tendency to selfishness, which is the very essence of sin and creates all those priceless ethical values of Brotherhood, which are essential to the founding of the Kingdom of God among men. These are the fundamental spiritual principles of Guild Socialism which translates them into economic expression under such terms as self-government in industry, national ownership, and democratic control; vocational direction of labour and functional claims to property. These suggest an organization of industry which will cultivate those co-operative virtues that are essential to brotherhood, and which will provide the atmosphere in which our Faith may find its full social and economic expression.

The doom of a Godless civilization is sealed. "Because that knowing God, they glorified Him not as God, neither gave thanks. . . . God gave them up." Because "they exchanged the truth of God for a lie, and worshipped and served the creature rather than the Creator . . . God gave them up." "Even as they refused to have God in their knowledge, God gave them up" (Romans i. 21). Human society organized apart from God is swiftly moving to the suicide of the human race in a universal war.

We believe that the Church in her Catholic complex of dogma, discipline, and devotion, in her social principles of faith, freedom, and fellowship has the only secret of man's redemption in binding men together into a living Fellowship with God. If she will purge herself from worldliness, idolatry, and selfishness and stake her life on establishing the Kingdom of God among men; if she will issue forth from the sanctuary to claim for Christ the absolute dominion over the whole life of man, to enthrone Him as King over our social relationships and our industrial and commercial activities, as well as over our individual life; if she will concentrate all her energies at whatever cost on giving social and economic expression to her Faith, then Christ will return to reign over us and "the kingdom of the world will become the Kingdom of our Lord and of his Christ."

EPILOGUE

BY
G. K. CHESTERTON

EPILOGUE

LAST night, as the grey twilight deepened into darkness, a weird and telepathic conviction came to me that somebody was somewhere at that moment writing down these words: "The modern world is no longer in the swaddling-bands of the creeds; it has come to years of discretion and claims a full responsibility for its own thoughts and actions"; or words to that effect. This conviction was not wholly due to a cold and creeping shudder that came across me; such as that which is said to warn a man that someone steps across his grave. It was indirectly connected with a conviction closer to experience; the knowledge that somebody does write that sentence every night in order, that it may appear every morning in all those newspapers which pride themselves on giving us what is new. But there is something much more extraordinary about that sentence than the suggestion that it is new; and that is the belated realization that came to me that, after all, it is true. I had read it some nine hundred and ninety times before it even occurred to me that this could be the case; but when I read it the nine hundred and ninety-first time I realized suddenly that, even in a world of so much seeming waste, even these words had not been written in vain. The phrase is much more true than the writers are aware; it is true in a sense that they would not at all approve; and if they knew how true it was, they probably would not write it. I confess that there falls on me a sort of hush

of awe, and almost of terror, to think of all those
thousands of journalists simultaneously writing down
something that is perfectly true, even without knowing it.

In a simple and almost sinister sense the modern
world really has come of age. That modern spirit that
had birth in the Renaissance, its boyhood in the Protes-
tant and commercial centuries, and its first manhood amid
the machinery of the industrial revolution, really has
been going long enough by this time to be judged on its
own merits. It really is old enough to take the responsibility for its own actions. It really is old enough to
answer for itself. But the fact may perhaps appear
less boisterously exhilarant when we consider what it
has to answer for, and what its actions have been.

In any case, however, the distinction is of some importance; because those who make this suggestion generally also make suggestions flatly inconsistent with it.
While insisting that the modern man can do anything
he likes, because it happens to be something they like,
they commonly take refuge in a contrary suggestion
when it happens to be something they do not like. Anything which is wrong with the world is attributed to the
stringency of those dogmatic bonds that have been burst
asunder, or the vitality of those superstitions that have
been finally slain. Now it is obvious that these philosophers cannot have it both ways. If it be true that emanci-
pated man has made a new and wonderful world in his
own image, he cannot possibly excuse the ugliness of the
image he has made, as due to his devotion to the idols
he has deserted. In short, if he is responsible for his
actions, he is responsible for his bad actions; and cannot
put the blame on the religion from which he broke away
in order to act at all. This is obvious even in abstract
logic, and much more vividly obvious when we come to

concrete facts. We may like or dislike modern machinery; but we cannot say it is a historical fact that a
modern machine was modelled on a torture-engine of the
Spanish Inquisition. We may like or dislike a hive of
workers "living in" under capitalist conditions; but we
cannot say it is a historical fact that those who arranged
it modelled it, with devout ardour, on a mediæval mon-
astery. We may like or dislike a modern colonial war;
but we cannot assert that it was imposed on us by the
Pope like a Crusade; we may like or dislike the Yellow
Press, but we cannot pretend that it is one of the false
colours flown by the Scarlet Woman. Modern man is,
as his admirers say, by this time a sufficiently ancient
man to have done a good many things on his own account,
without the slightest consultation with his mediæval
grandmother. There is hardly a link left of the chains
that bound him to the pre-reformation prison. He has
come out of prison long ago. The only question is what
has come out of prison; and whether some perverse persons have not been tempted to prefer the prison to the
prisoner.

In trying to judge this fairly, it may be well to begin
even with the simplest and most self-evident proviso;
that this normal question concerns the mass of mankind.
It would be as absurd to talk as if all mediæval men were
as wise and happy as the saints, as it would be to talk as
if all the modern men were as stupid and squalid as the
millionaires. Even to the chance examples already
chosen the application of this popular test holds good.
If we were simply comparing the machinery of the
Industrial Revolution with the machinery of the Inquisition, most of us would prefer even a threshing-machine
to a thumb-screw. But most men, even in the last and
worst days of the Inquisition, went to their graves

without knowing any more about the thumb-screw than most American citizens know about the Third Degree, and much less than they know about the ceremonial of burning negroes alive. On the other hand, no man can go to his grave, or go to his shop or his office, without knowing all about the good or evil of modern machinery. We can therefore, truly ask what the modern machinery has done with the mass of men; we might almost put it in the form of asking how it has manufactured the mass of men. And that comparison, though full of complexities like all historical things, is capable of a certain large simplification. The modern change found the mass of men living on the land, and it turned them out on to the road. It is quite true that they were originally called slaves on the land and were later called free men on the road; and we will give all due importance to such names. The road may be a symbol of liberty and the furrow of slavery; but the object here is to sum up the realities that were so symbolized. The point is that the modern spirit, as such, certainly did not tend to make the serf in the field the master of the field; but only to make him the master of the feet with which he walked in his freedom along the king's highway. He could only take his chance of selling his labour to this man or that; and I do not undervalue the fact that it was in form a free contract, even when it was in fact a leonine contract. But it certainly is the fact that his economic position as a modern wage-earner is less secure even than his position when he was a feudal serf, and far less dignified than when he had the luck to be a free guilds-man. If I say that there is at least a doubt, touching the mass of men, whether their lot has been improved at all by the vast rational revolution of the last four hundred years, I am deliberately adopting a tone of restraint and even of understatement. For I wish to emphasize the fact that all people who think, and not merely our own school of thinkers, have by this time reached that degree of doubt. Nobody is certain that Capitalism has been a success; nobody is certain that Industrialism can solve its own problems; nobody is certain that these problems were not solved better in the ages of faith. The revolution has revolved; the wheel has come full circle; the world has run its own course. And the world itself is doubtful of its goal. The world itself has lost its way. There is in it a doubt far deeper than what is commonly called religious doubt. It might be called irreligious doubt; or a doubt about the ideal wisdom even or irreligion. The Church, being an object of faith, is in some sense naturally an object of doubt. But modern men are not merely in doubt about what they believe, but about what they know. They are not merely questioning what they are told to do; they are questioning what they have done. What they have done is to destroy charity for the sake of competition, and then to turn their own competition into monopoly. What they have done is to turn both peasants and guildsmen into the employed, and then turn these into the unemployed. They trampled on a hundred humanities of piety and pity in order to rush after Free Trade; and their Free Trade has been so free that it has brought them within a stride of the Servile State. They gave up their shrines and their sacred hostels to the pleasure of an aristocracy, only to find that their aristocracy no longer consisted of aristocrats, or even of gentlemen. They have laid the world waste with the dreariest and most abject atheism, only to find that their very atheism has cleared a space for the return of the most fantastic superstitions of crystals and mascots. They have built a city of houses only notable for the size of the ground-rent and the smallness of the ground-plan; a city of whose wealth and poverty they are alike ashamed; a city from which they themselves flee into the country, and which they themselves cannot prevent from crawling outwards into the country to pursue them. But upon all these things the modern man looks doubtfully and with a double mind; for they are the fulfilments of his own doctrines of science and free thought; and it would be strange if some broken and half-forgotten sentence did not sometimes begin to form itself in his mind. "Unless the Lord built. . . ."

To the modern man who has reached this degree of real doubt, truer and more terrible than the cheap riddles of the Bible-smasher, the essays of this book are addressed. It would be, indeed, unwise to end it in a tone which denies that his doubt is a real doubt; that is, a doubt that cuts both ways. He may justly claim much that is valuable in the modern world; nor need he fear, as I think he sometimes does, that its critics propose merely an artificial and antiquarian reconstruction of the mediæval world. For, indeed, those who understand the Catholic tradition of Christianity are not offering a Church which is exclusively at issue with modern things, or even one that was exclusively expressed in mediæval things. The point is not so much that that age was relatively right while this age is relatively wrong; it is rather that the Church was relatively right when all ages were relatively wrong. Even if the modern man's doubt goes no farther than balancing sweating against serfdom, or swindling financiers against robber barons, it will imply the need of some third thing, some authority above the ages, to hold the balance. History has produced only one thing that can even claim to hold it.

When the Christian apostle declared that he died daily, he told all the truth there was in what was told us, in our youth, to the effect that the Church was dying. If the saint had died every day, the Church has died in every century. Many said the Church was dying when Julian proclaimed from the Imperial throne the worship of Apollo. Many would have said again, after the first triumphs of many oriental heresies, that the Church was dying; and in this sense they would have been right. The Church was dying; but the worship of Apollo was dead. Many would have said it when Calvinism was overshadowing province after province, and rightly; the Church was dying, but the oriental heresies were dead. When the French Revolution had made a new heaven and a new earth, it was quite obvious to every clear-sighted person that Christianity had come to an end. The Church was certainly dying; but Calvinism was dead. The Christian religion has died daily; its enemies have only died. And what we see before us to-day is not a mere fashion of the praise of one century over another; but at most a rather unique illustration of the fact that the world fares worse without that religion than with it. The Church is dying as usual; but the modern world is dead; and cannot be raised save in the fashion of Lazarus.